Y0-BOB-498

Break FREE
from **Burnout**
in **30 Days!**

SECRETS OF A
BURNOUT SURVIVOR

MARY LEWIS

Life Renovations
Scotts Valley, California

Copyright © 2002, Mary P. Lewis. All rights reserved.

Published by The Marketing Clinic under its imprint, Life Renovations.

No part of this book may be reproduced, or stored in a retrieval system, used or transmitted in any form or by any means, electronic or mechanical, including, but not limited to photocopying, digitized media or recording in any manner whatsoever without written permission of the author, except in the case of brief quotations embodied in critical articles and reviews given with appropriate copyright ownership attribution. For information, please contact:

The Marketing Clinic
245M Mt. Hermon Rd., #209
Scotts Valley, CA 95066
1-866-MARY-LEWIS (phone) • 831-438-3361 (fax)
email: info@maryplewis.com

Cover and interior design by Lightbourne
Book cover writing by Susan Kendrick
Creative editing by Deanna Brady

Edition   1 2 3 4 5 6 7 8 9 10

Publisher's Cataloging-in-Publication
(Provided by Quality Books. Inc.)

Lewis, Mary, 1956-
      Break free from burnout in 30 days : secrets of a
  burnout survivor / Mary Lewis. -- 1st ed.
            p. cm.
            Includes bibliographical references and index.
            LCCN 2002091286
            ISBN 0-9714237-0-9

      1. Burn out (Psychology) I. Title.

BF481.L49 2002   158.7'23
                                        QBI02-200371

Printed in the United States of America.
This book is printed on acid free paper.

This publication is sold with the understanding that the author and the publisher are not engaged in rendering legal, medical, psychological, accounting, or other professional services. If medical advice or other expert assistance is required or desired, the services of a competent professional person should be sought.

Dedication

To Allan Lewis:
teacher, husband, lover, soul mate, father
and Master Coach

Your love, wisdom, encouragement, and generosity
let me chart my course,
put the wind in my sails,
provisioned my voyages,
and demonstrated how
to be the captain of my own ship.

Contents

Acknowledgements

This book would not have been possible if it weren't for the following people, who have deeply influenced my life. I wish to express my heartfelt gratitude and appreciation. I can't mention everyone, for that would take a tome in itself. For those who don't see their names here and know they should be, it's not because you're not important to me but because my internal index file has been corrupted.

- Lorraine and Andy Planding, the best parents any kid could ever have had.

- Allan Lewis, my dear husband, who both demands and makes it possible that I fulfill my life's purpose.

- Gabrielle Windlow, my sister, who taught me how to walk a mile in someone else's shoes.

- Judy Irving, my coach, who helps me be the best coach I can be.

- Thomas Leonard, creative genius and coach, for his inspiration, wisdom, "edge," and boundless generosity in sharing his learning through

Coachville.com, and for being the inspiring model that he is.

- Madeleine Homan, friend and coach, for her insights, belief in me, love and "sailor's mouth" that says what I need to hear to when I need it most.

- Melon Dash, founder of the Transpersonal Swimming Institute and coach *extraordinaire*, for taking me beyond my 40+ years fear of being in deep water to become a certified open-water scuba diver, joyously playing with dolphins, manta rays, deep sea turtles, and Moray eels. It is her genius and dedication that showed me how to overcome fear everywhere in my life, not just in deep water!

- Susan Moreschi, coach, friend, and retreat partner, for her unwavering support and love.

- All my past and current clients, who continually challenge me to be my best at all times and whom I cherish for everything they've taught me. You know who you are!

- Penny Jackson, Jenne Holmgren, and Kirk Shorte for loving me enough to kick me in the butt when necessary and for seeing in me what I so often missed.

- Vera Kark, web design genius, for her friendship, belief in my writing ability, love, and boundless creativity.

- All my R&D Team members who helped me clarify content and encouraged me to bring forth my own special style, with special thanks to: Schuyler Morgan, Allison Summers, Elena Falken, Carolyn André, Kerri Kraft, Tasha Kostantacos, Senan Taylor, Nicki Riedel, Pam Martin, Gayle Uchida, Rob Huston, and Holly Green.

- My colleagues in the ICF: Judy Feld, Schuyler Morgan, Skip Borst, Ellen Walker, Lenore Mewton, Scott Wintrip, Bryan Webber, and Vivienne Powell, for their support and friendship.

- The incredibly talented coach-instructors of Coach University for helping me continuously to hone my coaching talents and skills, especially Helene Van Manen, Barbara Luther, Karen Whitworth, Phil Cohen, and Edie Pereira-Hulbert.

- Dan Bellack for pointing me in the right direction in my career development: "Mary, trouble-shooting businesses and other people's lives is what you do best. Now if you could only make a living at it…."

- John Baird, professor and executive coach, for first pointing out to me how fearless and good I was at asking the hard questions no one else would.

- Anne Sanquini, Lou Hoffman, Alan Kerr for your friendship, your advice, your teaching, your caring.

- Jezebel, Gideon, Quan-Yin, my four-footed furry

companions whose purring, unconditional love, and playfulness improve my coaching and writing.

- A very special thanks to my publishing team: Deanna Brady, a talented editor, who has made me sound so much more articulate and logical. Susan Kendrick, a phenomenal copywriter, who took these concepts to heart and wrote them more compellingly than I ever dared dream. And lastly to Shannon Bodie of Lightbourne, a brilliant and delightful designer, who turned my vision of an attractive and pleasurable-to-read book into a reality.

- Marti Simanek, Danny Toback, Mary Gooch-Wallis, Barbara Planding, Mary W. Planding, Malachi the Wise, dear friends and unwavering supporters, who have gone ahead to prepare a warm welcome for me when it's my turn to leave this earth.

Preface

To know when you have enough is to be rich beyond measure.
—Lao Tzu

As a veteran marketing professional and a survivor of the high-tech and dotcom industries, I burned out not once, not twice, but *three times*. It took hitting the wall on the third occasion before I finally accepted that what I was doing was an exercise in futility. To keep doing the same things over and over and expecting a different result is one definition of insanity, isn't it?

Back then, "burnout" was not a widely recognized term or condition. There were no such people as professional coaches (at least, none that I knew of). There were therapists, there were career counselors, there were other "burnouts"; but there was no one I could turn to who could provide the clarity, support, and structures I so desperately needed to turn my life around. It seemed I had to figure this out on my own.

My journey from high-tech burnout to successful professional coach took ten arduous years of working mostly on my own. The biggest lesson I learned from that experience was that while pain may be inevitable, *suffering is definitely optional.*

I wrote this book to help you stop suffering from burnout, ASAP. I want to share with you the secrets of my clients' and my success so you don't have to suffer any more.

This is not a pipe dream. ***You can do this!*** I've been working successfully with clients for the past four years, and I've seen them **break free** from the cycle and go on to **live wonderful, successful, happy lives.** If they can, if I can...***you can, too!***

Make this book your trusty companion, and let it give you a helping hand out of the abyss in which you find yourself or help you avoid burnout completely.

May you hear what your heart speaks and find the courage to follow it.

Blessings,

Mary Lewis
Scotts Valley, CA
January 2002

Top 10 Signs of Burnout

Check "Y' if the statement describes you most of the time, check "N" if it does not. Give yourself 1 point for each Y. Total up the number of "Y"s to get your score. See next page for the Scoring Scale.

Y   N

___ ___ I usually set my alarm way before I have to get up, then continue to pound the snooze button before I finally stumble out of bed, still feeling exhausted, frantic that now I am late for work.

___ ___ I am either one of the first folks out the door at the end of the workday feeling as though I have just escaped from jail or else I feel like a mole (arriving at work before dawn and leaving in the wee hours of the night).

___ ___ People more often than not ask me if I'm feeling ok, even when I'm not sick.

___ ___ I dread Mondays and live for Fridays, holidays, and long weekends because I rarely take time off.

___ ___ I do not care how I treat customers or colleagues, I just do not have the energy to deal with them.

___ ___ I cannot remember the last time I felt a sense of pride or accomplishment at the end of a workday.

___ ___ I am in a constant state of feeling overwhelmed. I rarely feel that I make any progress no matter how much I do or how hard I work.

___ ___ I make cynical remarks and jokes about my firm and I do not care who hears me.

___ ___ I lose my temper more easily than I ever have before and when I do, it feels great just to let it erupt, even if it was only over something minor.

___ ___ The whole thought of looking for another job leaves me cold. I just can't face going through that ordeal all over again.

___ ___ **TOTAL**

Scoring Scale

1—3 points
SMOLDERING

You are experiencing mild stress on the job. It could just be a temporary situation remedied by better self-care such as exercise, healthful eating and R&R. This is the perfect time to work with a coach to create your self-care program. If exhaustion has been a major factor for more than a month, consider seeing a sleep disorder specialist. A huge percentage of Americans suffer from sleep disorders and do not know it. Sleep disorders do more than just rob you of needed rest—some can potentially end your life, such as sleep apnea.

4—5 points
CAMPFIRE

Dis-stress is growing and if not dealt with can quickly begin to consume all your energy. This is a great time to work with a coach to remove energy drains, set standards and boundaries in your work and home life and to expand your self-care program.

6—8 points
4-ALARM FIRE

The Universe has been sending you messages, which

you have not heard and you are now in crisis mode. This is an ideal time to work with a coach to: identify those messages you've been missing, get clear on what is really important to you, set goals to get out of crisis, create reserves in energy, space, time, money, etc.

9—10 points
BURNED OUT

Recommend you immediately review your physical and mental health—see a physician and/or a therapist to get treatment for potential problems such as sleep disorders, hormone and chemical imbalances, addictions, depression, etc. This is an excellent time to work with a coach to take actions for extreme self-care and to get clarity, structure, and support in rebuilding a happier, healthier personal and professional life. The question now becomes NOT do you have the time, and/or the funds, to see a specialist and/or a coach, but rather will you STILL HAVE the body, mind, health, family, and ability to earn if you do not.

Introduction

***When you find yourself in a hole,
the first thing to do is stop diggin'.***
—Will Rogers

What Exactly Is Burnout?

Burnout is most often defined as physical and/or emotional exhaustion, especially as a result of long-term stress or dissipation. In the arenas of medicine, research, psychology, and occupational health, it is known by various names, such as *job stress, work stress, job burnout,* etc.

The Burnout Cycle

It's been my experience that burnout is often a cycle. It is a combination of behaviors that are repeated over and over again. I have come up with a diagram that I believe best illustrates what I call " The Burnout Cycle" (see fig. 1 on the following page).

There are three ways you might enter the burnout cycle. It can start with anger, exhaustion, or pain.

Once any two of those elements are present at the same time, the cycle can begin.

Let's look at the cycle's ingredients:

- When you are *pain* and are *exhausted*, you will most likely take *little or no action*. An example might be that you avoid confronting an employee about poor work quality, or you don't do your laundry or you don't discipline your kids.
- When you are *exhausted* and *angry*, you have a tendency to *react* immediately, without thought for the consequences of your actions. For instance, your kids are fighting in the back seat of the car, and you automatically snap at them.

The Burnout Cycle

- When you are *angry* and in *pain*, you *overreact*. An example might be that a customer calls you to complain about a product, and you immediately overreact by arguing vehemently with them and then slam down the phone.

Exhaustion is the result of a *depletion* of your emotional, physical, intellectual, and spiritual *needs*.

Pain is the result of *violations* to your emotional, physical, intellectual, and spiritual *boundaries* and *standards*.

Anger is the result of *self-deception,* when you are denying your physical, emotional, intellectual, and spiritual *truths*.

If you are burned out, you are experiencing all three of these conditions every day of every week of every month, either simultaneously or in sequence. You bounce from doing nothing to totally losing it for no apparent reason. You feel out of control and often experience moments of wondering who the heck this person is whom you observe saying and doing all these things. It doesn't *feel* like you, yet it *is* you saying and doing them. This has probably been going on for months (and in some cases for years). In fact, it may have been going on so long that you are unable to remember when or how the cycle started, or even why.

I'm not talking about isolated incidents or occasional days here and there; we all have strenuous days from time to time that leave us drained. I am describing someone who lives this way on a daily basis and has probably done so over the years in various iterations (jobs, relationships, etc.).

The first thing you probably did to try to resolve this condition was to take a long vacation, thinking that all you needed was some R&R. You probably *did* need some R&R, and the vacation helped your body to recover. It simply wasn't enough to break the burnout cycle, and you realized that it was not the *whole* answer because a week after your return you felt like you had never even gone!

Then you probably thought the problem was the job or your manager or your company or your romantic partner...and if only you had a better job or worked for a better or different company or had a different manager or partner, the problem would be solved. So you found that new position or firm or partner, only to discover a few months later that you were right back in the bloody rut again.

You sort of saw it coming, but you've been trying to ignore it until now—when you are so deep in the hole that you think you're going completely crazy.

You feel helpless, frustrated, out of control, hurt, desperate, and disillusioned. You wonder things like, "Why *me*? How did I ever *get* here? Why do I *always* seem to work my butt off and go nowhere? How come this always happens *to me*? Why can't I ever seem to find the *right* job (or company or partner)? What's *wrong* with me? What's wrong with the *world*? Is life really just a bitch, and then you die?"

You have begun to believe that this is how your life was destined to be—that in order to make a decent living or be "successful," you have to suffer and drive yourself into the ground until you have nothing left to give. So you chalk it up as the price you have to pay. You figure you've got to live with it, just suck it up. For you, the thought of creating and living a life that you love is only a laughable pipedream.

What Is the Dream?
My guess is that you want to feel free—*truly free*—for the first time in your life that you can remember clearly. This diagram (figure 2 on the following page) captures what it is that I believe you hunger for. (Don't worry if the ingredients don't seem to fit you right now. Just go with this for the moment.)

When you have an *abundance* of everything you need in your life (whatever those needs might be) and you are acting with and from *integrity*, *joy* is the result.

When you act in full *authenticity* (an absence of self-deception) and have an *abundance* of all that you need, *serenity* appears.

When you act with and from *integrity* and in full *authenticity*, *truth* emerges.

The Freedom Cycle

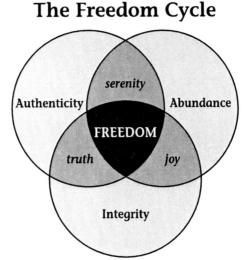

So why is this important?

When these three elements are present in your life, you now have the freedom to

- be or not to be whomever you want.
- do or not to do whatever you want
- have or not to have whatever you want

That sure feels like freedom to me! What does freedom feel like to you? (Feel free to copy the diagram format and rewrite the text, using words that work for you.)

It's Not A Pipedream

I'm here to tell you that creating and living a life you love does not have to be a pipedream. Staying burned out is a **choice**. If being burned out gives you pleasure, then give this book the heave-ho, and ignore me. (Believe it or not, there are quite a few people out there who actually love being burned out—even though they don't realize it.) But if you choose to join me on this journey and break free from burnout, you *must* be ready, willing, and able.

Right now, the last thing you need is to feel like you have failed. To keep that from happening, please answer the following questions "yes" or "no."

Y / N

Are You Ready?

_____ Have you decided that you will not suffer anymore?

_____ Have you decided that, instead of being paralyzed, you want to take some concrete, tangible actions to change things for the better, even if you may not quite know what those actions are?

_____ Have you decided that you no longer want to feel or be trapped?

_____ Have you decided that you want to stop stagnating and start growing again?

Are You Willing?

_____ Will you try almost anything to improve your life, even if it seems stupid, weird, or totally unrelated to your goal?

_____ Will you suspend judgment long enough to let yourself experience something new?

_____ Will you do the necessary tasks requested of you, regardless of what else is going on in your life?

_____ Will you do whatever it takes to stop and/or change the behaviors that you discover are getting in your way?

Are You Able?

_____ Will you refuse to let mistakes stop you?

_____ Can you persevere despite not seeing instant, tangible results?

_____ Do you have the courage to let go of beliefs, people, places, and things that hinder you?

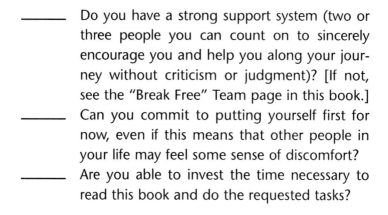

_____ Do you have a strong support system (two or three people you can count on to sincerely encourage you and help you along your journey without criticism or judgment)? [If not, see the "Break Free" Team page in this book.]

_____ Can you commit to putting yourself first for now, even if this means that other people in your life may feel some sense of discomfort?

_____ Are you able to invest the time necessary to read this book and do the requested tasks?

If you have answered "No" to three or more questions, put down this book. Wait a month or two, and do whatever preliminary work you need so that you can answer these questions with fewer than three No's.

If you have answered "Yes" to at least eleven questions, please turn the page and join me in breaking free!

The Perfect Place

> ***No snowflake ever falls***
> ***in the wrong place.***
> —Zen Saying

You're in the Perfect Place

"Since when?" you exclaim. "I'm miserable, I'm tired, I don't feel up to doing anything. How can you possibly say I'm in the perfect place? *This* is *perfect?*"

Yep. In spite of how that sounds right now, it's true.

I understand completely why you feel the way you do. I've been there myself, and it feels awful. You're practically numb from stress and exhaustion. You sometimes think it will never end. You can't tell one day from another anymore, and most of the time you just don't care. You hardly know why you bother getting up every day, and you probably wouldn't if you didn't have to earn money to pay your bills or care for your family.

Congratulations! If you have read this far, it means

11

you have made a decision that you *want out* of being *burned out*.

It took a lot of courage to reach this point! I'm excited for you because you are moving on and grabbing for the life you have always wanted.

That's perfect.

You Have Hit Bottom

Since you've obviously hit bottom, there's no place else to go but up. (I can hear you groaning.)

Seriously...you haven't got anything to lose at this point, right? What more *perfect* place to be than in a *no-lose* situation?

Missed Messages

You are where you are for a reason. Although you may not have realized it, the Universe (or a higher being, or the Divine, or the collective soul—whatever you want to call it) has been sending you messages, and you haven't been listening. By not heeding these messages, you have allowed symptoms of burnout (exhaustion, ill temper, apathy, despair, etc.) to develop and worsen. As you continued to disregard these signals, the symptoms got worse and worse until now you are here—in a full-fledged crisis. You are burning out or have already burned out completely.

Perfect. Now you can rise like a phoenix from the ashes!

Opportunities for Learning

There are many useful things to be learned from burning out—things you couldn't learn anywhere else except along this path you are on. Now you'll get a chance to understand what you have missed before and will learn new things. You'll also make sure to heed those messages right away next time!

You *need* to be here right now. How perfect! That's why you are in "the Perfect Place."

CLEAN UP YOUR ACT

No Victims Here — No More Whining

I'm going to say some things right now that you may find hard to swallow. Please know that I say these things lovingly, with care and compassion. They need to be said because you need to hear them in order for things to change for the better.

You, and you alone, got you into this place. No one put you here. No one made you do anything you didn't want to do (even though it may not feel like that right now). No one made your decisions for you. Each decision you made brought you closer and closer to where you find yourself right now, in this very moment. What's that old saying? "You made your bed, now lie in it."

What you just read may have hurt—even a lot—

but please don't give up on me yet. Stick with me a little longer, and keep reading.

You can't change the past. Right now, you need to stop beating yourself up about what you could have or should have done differently or better. Remember the saying, "What's done is done"?

Please understand that I am *not* berating you or saying you were inept. *Absolutely not!*

You did the best you could at the time!

I *am* saying that there were always options available to you, even if you may not have liked them very much and even if you didn't see them all. You just weren't equipped to make better choices for yourself. You did the very best you could with what you had to work with at the time.

Now, it's time to wipe your slate clean, forgive yourself, and recommit to *you*.

Now is the time to become aware and gather all the available tools and resources so that in the future you can make *choices* instead of *decisions*.

Decisions are what you make when you feel boxed in and pressured, with seemingly limited options. *Choices* are what you make when you have an abundance of space, time, and other resources, with limitless options.

I want you always to make choices, not decisions.

To do that, you need to take *ownership* of your past decisions. You need to stop any whining you've been doing, or blaming anyone or anything else for your predicament. It's unproductive and keeps you right where you are now—and as "perfect" as this place may be, do you really want to stay here?

When you can finally say, "Yes, *I* decided to work eighty hours a week," or "*I* took that job knowing I'd hate my boss," and/or whatever else *you* decided—you will be on your way to beating burnout. You will be ready to decipher the messages sent to you so you don't miss them again, and you will be ready to create the space and time you need so you can finally see all those limitless options that really do exist for you.

Will you wipe the slate clean and forgive yourself?
Will you recommit to yourself?
Will you take the actions you need to move forward and break free of stress and burnout?

> **REQUEST:** Put aside an hour today when you can be alone with your thoughts and not be interrupted. Make sure the environment is conducive to your being able to think without distractions.

Now, trace your journey backwards to discover how you arrived where you are now. What decisions did you make that led you here? No evading the truth!

If doing this by yourself is difficult, you might ask someone to interview you who can remain detached from your situation. Tape-record your discussion so neither of you has to take notes, and you can just focus on the conversation.

My purpose in asking you to do this is *not* for you to get out the cat-o'-nine-tails and start flagellating yourself! What I want is for you to discern the *patterns* in your decisions, in the situations you created for yourself, in what you did, or didn't do, what you felt, and what you thought that put you into this jail cell called **burnout**.

These patterns will give you a clue about behaviors and beliefs you may need to rethink and perhaps modify if they aren't working well for you anymore. You won't uncover them all in one sitting, but you'll make a good start. The more often you take time to think about all this, the clearer the patterns will become.

Each day for the next month, take one hour to be there for yourself. *This is your Sacred Hour*, when you take care of yourself and give yourself the space to ruminate, experiment, and play.

Capture your thoughts, insights, feelings, and ideas in a *Travel Log*. You are beginning your "burnout journey," and this Travel Log will become your faithful companion.

Your Travel Log can be on paper or electronic. It can be fancy, or it can be plain. You can write, paint, draw, paste pictures in it, doodle on it. You can also take photos or make videos or tape recordings. Use whatever it may be that lets you express yourself freely—have a blast! Think of this as a trip you are on during which you want to record your experiences so you can remember them effortlessly.

Get into the habit of carrying your Travel Log with you so you can jot down ideas or capture moments that are meaningful to you at any time they occur. *At minimum, get into the habit of recording one thought or feeling each day.*

After a month, you will be astounded when you look back to see what's happened!

Gag Your Inner Critic

I know worrying must be effective
because almost nothing I
worried about ever happened.
—Will Rogers

It seems that we all hear a monologue (or sometimes a dialogue) in our heads, a noisy little "monkey," a judgmental type of chatter that eats away at us. I call this my "Inner Critic." She (this gender identification is for ease of expression, not because I'm picking on women) is the accumulation of every single unloving, nasty, miserable, critical, obnoxious, cruel statement ever made to you by a parent, teacher, friend, spouse, lover, coworker, boss, sibling, relative, etc. Her sole purpose in life is to make you miserable because the more miserable and unhappy you are, the more energy she has to exist and the more power she has to continue to make you miserable.

Any time you hear in your head an *"oughta, shoulda, coulda, woulda"* statement, this is your Inner Critic, yakking away and making you feel like garbage. The last thing you want to do is start to argue with her, because the moment you begin to argue, you lose. By wrestling with her instead of doing more important, pleasurable things, you give her your attention, and that's what she lives for—to be on center stage, to distract you, and to be in control of her audience: *you.*

Gag her, and your life will become immeasurably better!

REQUEST: Begin to observe your Inner Critic. Listen with total objectivity and detachment. Don't fight with her; don't argue with her. Just observe her when she shows up. Notice what she is saying, and know that it is *she* who is saying it, not you.

Now you can consider what she has said. If she starts to scream, really rant, rave, and freak you out, just keep observing her. Don't allow yourself to react. Just watch and listen. Take deep, even breaths. Focus on feeling the breath moving in and out of your nostrils. Make your inhalations and exhalations the same length. Then begin to make your exhalations last even longer than your inhalations.

When you have calmed down and are no longer tense, choose what you want to do based on how *you feel* about it and what you think is right for you— regardless of her statements to you.

Simply noticing her in this way, without reacting to her, will be enough to gag her (if only for a short while). With practice, you'll be able to muzzle her more often and for longer periods of time. Now who's in control? *You!* Yippeee!

But beware...she's sneaky. She can change costumes, change personalities, change attitudes—all in an attempt to continue to make you miserable. So no matter how she's disguised herself, beware, and remember these three steps:

1) Notice her and what she says,
2) consciously choose to agree with her or not, then,
3) think/feel/be/do as *you* have chosen.

Draw a picture of her in your Travel Log, or just describe her. Your Inner Critic may have many faces. Name her and all her different personalities.

I call my Inner Critic "Wanda the Witch." Wanda dresses just like the Wicked Witch of the West in *The Wizard of Oz*—even looks a lot like her. She has that memorable, oily, cackling voice when she pretends to be my friend and then lets out that awful screech when I ignore her...or when she's trying to convince me that I'm going to die if I don't listen to her. When she's trying to be my friend, she dresses up like the Good Witch of the North, but her face and voice are so ugly that she can't fool me!

One day, I drew a picture of Wanda and put her up on a corkboard. Every time I heard what she said and then refused to do what she told me to, I threw another dart at the corkboard and imagined a bucket of water being thrown on her. I would then imagine watching her melt, and my smile would last for hours!

It felt really good.

In fact, it still does!

DAY 3

Get Healthy

Self-love, my liege, is not so vile a sin
As self-neglecting.
—William Shakespeare, Henry V

Your Number One priority is to get physically and emotionally fit. Whatever it takes to get you there, at the fastest pace you can welcome, is essential to breaking free from burnout.

You need to sleep well, eat well, and develop healthy self-care habits. You must build up your strength so that you have the desire and the energy to establish a foundation from which to make choices.

Self-Care

Self-care is making sure you get what you need to support your mind, body, heart, and spirit so you can live life with joy. This may take some time for you to get used to, since most of us are not accustomed to putting ourselves first. You will be amazed at the difference it will make when you practice self-care regularly. The longer most people follow a self-care program that they've custom-built for themselves, the more they report feeling stronger, better, happier, clearer, more "centered," and more relaxed.

Taking care of yourself is not the same thing as being vain or self-centered. It is *not* a fad or a trend. Self-care takes courage, practice, persistence, and self-love. It is *crucial* to your long-term well being. In addition, it benefits others in your life. When you take care of yourself first, you have more to give over the long term.

REQUEST: Make a commitment to yourself to put your health and well-being first and to do whatever is necessary to take care of your physical and emotional wellness. Demonstrate that commitment now by doing the following during your sacred hour today:

Schedule a physical immediately if you have not had one in more than a year. This is especially important if you are experiencing exhaustion, lethargy, stomach upset or pain, chest pain, shortness of breath, non-refreshing sleep, joint pains, or depression.

Your health practitioner is always your best starting point. First make sure you have a health practitioner who really cares about you (or find one who does), and then tell him or her that you are struggling with feeling burned out and want to get healthy. He or she can help you pinpoint your physical (and sometimes your emotional) needs. If you describe what's going on, what you are doing, and why, your health practitioner can recommend a course of treatment—perhaps an exercise program suited to your state of health, a change in diet, even a specialist to see. Once you are treated physically, that will be one less thing on your mind, one less worry.

Do you find yourself automatically saying "I'm tired" every time anyone asks how you are? Do you wake up feeling tired more often than not, or you snore a great deal? If so, talk to your doctor about the situation, and discuss seeing a sleep-disorder specialist.

Sleep disorders and related sleep deprivation affect more than 75 million Americans today. This specialized branch of medicine has evolved exponentially and has developed many different ways to help you.

I spent thirty years without ever having a complete night of restful sleep, no matter how many hours I slept. (You can imagine what it was like being around me. If you looked up *nasty* in the dictionary, my picture was right there!) My sleep deprivation contributed enormously to my burnout and to feeling exhausted all the time.

One day my husband heard a sleep-disorders expert, Dr. William Dement, speaking on a talk-radio show, and my husband recognized in me much of what Dr. Dement described. I immediately contacted the Stanford Sleep Disorders Clinic. Now I wake up every day refreshed and full of energy because of their accurate diagnosis and the treatment that followed. If only I had known about all this sooner, my burnout might not have been as severe as it was. You don't have to go on depriving yourself of a good night's sleep, either!

You might also want to examine your bed, its bedding, the mattress and your bedroom. Do they create the most conducive environment to sleep in? Is the mattress in good condition and the right firmness for you? If it isn't, go buy the right one for you!

Is the bedding comfortable or is it time to finally get the right sheets, pillows, blankets, etc. that let you sleep comfortably (cotton and flannel are natural fibers that support and work with your body's temperature changes). Is the room the right temperature for you? (Open a window, add a blanket, turn on a fan, etc.) Is the room too light? Is it sufficiently quiet? What about blinds, curtains to muffle light and sound? Are you allergic to dust or mold? Dust and vacuum regularly and eliminate the source of any dampness that fosters the growth of mold. Also buy the appropriate mattress, pillow, and comforter covers that prevent dust mites from moving in!

For more information look under *"Sleep"* in *Resources*.

In your Travel Log, record how much time you spend every day doing various tasks. Most people find it convenient to make a table like the example below. (This may feel somewhat awkward and weird at first, and I'm asking you to trust me that it will be worthwhile.)

	S	M	T	W	T	F	S
Sleeping	9	8	8	8	8	8	9
Commuting	-	1	1	1	1	1	-
Work	-	9	8	8	9	8	-
Eating	3	1	1	1	2	3	3
Dressing	1	1	1	1	1	1	1
Laundry	-	-	2	-	2	-	2
Shopping	-	-	-	1	-	-	-
Kid-limo	-	1	-	1	-	1	1
Girl Scouts	-	2	-	-	-	-	-
House-cleaning	3	1	1	1	1	1	3
Yoga	2	-	1	-	1	-	2
Gardening	3	-	-	-	-	-	3
Subtotal	20	23	22	21	24	22	24
FREE TIME	**4**	**1**	**2**	**3**	**0**	**2**	**0**

At the end of day, add up the hours and subtract the subtotal from 24. The result is your "free time." Note anything interesting that you discover, any feelings you have, any surprises, etc.

We will revisit your Personal Time Chart on Day 9.

One Step At A Time

There is no terror in the bang,
only in the anticipation of it.
—Alfred Hitchcock

Whenever we attempt to make changes in our lives, somewhere along the way we often experience reactions ranging from twinges of anxiety to full-blown panic attacks. *Fear* can be our greatest enemy if we allow it to be, for it can reduce our ability to act. *Courage* is not the absence of fear but is the ability to act anyway, despite the fear we feel.

Fear is an emotional state that we create when we perceive ourselves to be in danger. The greater the perceived danger, the more debilitating the fear can be. And that's the key—*our perception.*

We manufacture our perceptions. What we *imagine* to be true *becomes* true for us, true in our own minds and bodies. We create our own reality. The good news is that we can control our perceptions, and we can therefore control our fear and "un-imagine" it too!

Imagine that your body is enveloped in a gossamer bubble. This bubble represents your essence, the intangible part of you that makes you unique. You just happen to reside in a physical package called a *body*. When your bubble, the essential energy that surrounds your body, is not filled with fear, you are more likely to say that you feel "grounded" or "centered."

Keep this picture in mind.

Let me give you an example of how we can create a reality of fear. For most of my life I was so afraid of drowning that, at the age of forty, I would not even get my face wet in the shower! This had been going on since I was four or five, and by forty, fear had infiltrated nearly every aspect of my life, pretty much debilitating me completely. Here are the thoughts and feelings I had when I was learning to overcome my fear of water.

It is the day before my first swim-coaching session. I'm in bed, warm, and feeling centered and grounded and safe. I realize that the next day is *the* day, and I stop thinking about it before I start to get nervous. (My bubble is completely surrounding my body.)

Now I am in my car, driving to my first swim-coaching session. I am feeling a bit anxious because I keep thinking about being in the pool. My hands and feet are freezing, and I start to shiver and I turn up the heater. I start thinking about not going and almost turn around. (My bubble has shrunk a little, so my hands and feet are exposed.)

I'm with my coach and the group during our discussion time, and I'm starting to feel kind of shaky. When it is over, I have a hard time standing up because I keep thinking about going into the water. (My bubble has lifted to where it is now above my knees.)

I am in the dressing room, changing into my swimming suit. I am really getting nervous because I can hear the echoing of people's voices out in the pool area, and all I can think is *What if one of them pushes me in?* I am ready to throw up. The butterflies in my stomach are whirling like mad! (My bubble has lifted just above my rib cage.)

I am standing by the side of the pool, near the steps. I feel like I cannot breathe, and my heart is pounding. I can barely put one foot in front of the other. I keep seeing myself drowning. I know it is absurd to feel this way with so many people around to rescue me, but it doesn't matter. (My bubble is now just below my throat.)

My coach asks me to step into the water, just on the first step in the shallow end. I can barely think about doing it. I cannot speak. In fact, I can't do it. I do not take that step. I am paralyzed. (My bubble is just under my nose.)

My coach says something to me, but I cannot hear her. In fact, I cannot hear or see anybody. There's just a roaring sound in my ears. I am hyperventilating. I can't get enough air. I can't seem to breathe. All I can see is me, floating on top of the water, dead. (My bubble is way above my head and away from my body.)

What was happening here? Did you catch it? Yes, my bubble kept shrinking and moving up and away from my body. Why was that? *Because I was picturing what was going to happen.* I was completely caught up in creating the future—a future in which I was dead. Wanda the Witch had been reminding me cheerfully at every turn that I was going to die if I went into the water.

For all intents and purposes, I was somewhere else. I certainly was not in that pool. I was too busy listening to Wanda feeding my fear and helping me to picture that I was already dead—a future *I* created.

I was not present.

Because I was not present, I was unable to see the control I had and what I could actually do.

To help me overcome my fear, my coach, Melon, had me break everything down into tiny, tiny, baby steps. First, I had to go to the edge of the pool and just stand there and look at the water. Then, she had me close my eyes and breathe deeply until I could feel my hands and feet again, until I could feel my knees stop shaking. As I did this, I began to feel how warm the air was on my skin, how moist it was, how strong the chlorine scent was. I could feel a slight draft, but instead of chilling me, it felt pleasant. I was becoming *present*.

Wanda actually shut up! I was no longer thinking about drowning. I was not even thinking about stepping into the water. I was simply being with my body at that moment. As I became present, I was in control, and I could see what choices were available to me. I could step into the water or not. In fact, I did not have to go into the water at all unless I wanted to and, to quote Melon, "… *only* if it sounds like fun!"

Now I was ready to take the next step. I stepped into the water up to my ankles. She instructed me to pay attention to what I was feeling, to stop the moment I felt uncomfortable, and to focus on the part of my body that was in contact with the water. I felt the water caress my toes as it lapped up and down my ankles in rhythm to the movement of everyone else in the pool. It felt nice! I was okay.

I took another step. This time I was in up to my knees, a little more nervous because I could feel the water tugging at me. It was stronger. I stayed where I was and held on to the handrail. I could hear other people around me, but I ignored them. I focused on the way the water felt on my knees, and I kept breathing deeply. I was feeling pretty good. The water felt okay.

Then I took another step down, and this time the water covered my stomach. I gasped and leaped back up to the previous step. I had not expected the water to feel so cold. I stayed on that step, kept breathing, and waited until I recaptured my sense of calm. This time, I knew it would feel cold for a moment when I stepped down. I let that happen, holding on to the side of the pool. Some discomfort came back because I could feel the water pulling me. I was not afraid, merely uncomfortable because I was unfamiliar with the way the water felt.

For the first time in my life, I realized that *I was in control in the water* because I knew exactly what to do to make myself feel okay in the water. I could step back up as far back as I needed to. *Duh!*

This is an example of how to break something down into baby steps—to move forward when ready, and to go back if you've gone too far and then begin again once you've centered yourself.

Why have I spent so much time on this? Because we all feel fear, and I have found that fear is *the primary reason* why people get stuck, are stuck, and stay stuck!

When you encounter fear, I want you to remember this process to help you pass through your fear so you can act from *choice*.

As you go through this book, you will experience fear from time to time. Why? Because some of the things I'm going to ask you to play with may require you to make changes in how you look at things, how you do things, what you believe, or even who you have been.

Your "Wanda" does *not* want you to change, because then you will not need her anymore, and she'll be powerless. She isn't going to give up without a fight, so be prepared. When she fights, she fights dirty. Fear is her nastiest, most powerful weapon, and she won't hold back from using it.

Fear is a big reason why change can be difficult or even painful. However, growth can't occur without change. A sapling does not grow into a tree, a caterpillar change into a butterfly, a tadpole into a frog without massive change!

Massive change is what you're about to experience. You're in a jail cell right now, and it's labeled **burnout**. You're going to break out of jail and leap forward into this incredible life you are building for yourself! Wow! How truly exciting this is going to be for you!

You can do this! Just put one foot in front of the other, and take it one step at a time.

> **REQUEST:** Begin to notice whenever you feel anxiety— pounding heart, cold hands or feet, nervous stomach, difficulty breathing, etc. Try to catch it happening earlier and earlier in the process.

Whenever you notice any tension, no matter how small, *stop*.

Begin to breathe deeply, close your eyes (if you can do that safely), and become aware of the air as it passes through your nostrils. Feel your chest rise and fall, and become aware of the air on your face and the clothing on your body. Make your inhalations and exhalations the same length, then lengthen your exhalations so they are longer than your inhalations. All this will help you to center yourself and become fully present.

When you are totally aware of physical reality in the present moment, ask yourself, *What made me feel so frightened / anxious / tense?*

Once you clarify that, ask yourself, *What do I want to do?*

Choose what you truly want, and *then, only then,* respond to the situation.

In your Travel Log, record any situations in which you are frightened and what you do when that happens. What types of situations are they? What do they have in common?

Of what are you most afraid?

What baby steps can you take, perhaps moment by moment or day by day, to reduce your fear?

Write down those steps in your Travel Log, and when you will do them. As you do them, note down what you observe, what you feel, and what differences you are experiencing.

"No." Is a Complete Sentence

You have to decide what your highest priorities are and have the courage—pleasantly, smilingly, non-apologetically—to say "no" to other things. And the way you do that is by having a bigger "yes" burning inside.

—Stephen Covey

How many times have you said yes to doing something, only to want to kick yourself in the butt the moment the words left your mouth? You will do well to think about why you say *yes* when you really want to say *no*. Are you trying to impress people or be liked by them? Are you afraid you'll lose your job, be blamed or ignored? Maybe it's to win points, be appreciated, be rewarded? Also be sure to notice what Wanda is telling you.

Since time is a nonrenewable resource, and you are incapable of being in more than one place at a time, there are limits to how many things your body / heart / mind / soul can do all at once.

How many times has that *yes* meant that you didn't get to see your kids in their school play? You did not take your vacation? You did not see your dentist? You did not have that massage you were so looking forward to? You did not spend a quiet evening at home with your loved one(s) or in blissful, renewing solitude? You did not sleep well or long enough that night?

You need to consider where you really want to be spending your time and your energy. You need to free up space in your life so that you can do what you really want to. This is why I want you to be aware of a certain inescapable aspect of life:

When you say *yes* to one thing, you are unavoidably saying *no* to something else.

If you are truly burned out, you need to take drastic action. If you don't, your health will continue to suffer, and so will your career and your personal life. **If you are really *fed up* and no longer want to be burned out, you must be ready, willing, and able to make significant changes in your life.**

The first time I burned out, I did not truly comprehend or appreciate just how fried I really was. I was so burned that after asking to be laid off, I sat in my living room for most of the next six weeks, doing *absolutely nothing* but staring out the window at my garden. All I could manage was to buy groceries, do the laundry, take a shower, and eat. Pay bills? Ha! I had the money, just not the energy. I would not even answer the phone because talking with anyone took a seemingly superhuman effort that I didn't possess. I thought that all I needed was to sleep, rest, relax, take things easy.

That strategy handled the physical part of my burnout. It did not do quite as much for the emotional, spiritual, and intellectual aspects. I knew that I was merely existing, not living. You see, Wanda was filling up my head with all kinds of garbage. Despite her efforts, however, I knew deep inside that there had to be a better way to live.

When Burnout Number Two came along, it hit me hard—really hard. I wound up in the hospital because I had abused my health. Fortunately, my condition was not fatal, and I recovered completely. Since I had again asked to be laid off, I was also then out of work. I had met my housing goals previously and was living near the ocean (with a mortgage payment of $3000 a month). In that financial situation, I didn't have much time. I needed to find a new job, and fast.

At that point I was determined that I was never going to be burned out again. I began taking drastic measures, the same measures I am asking you to take. They were not easy, and they were not always fun. They forced me to face some things about myself I hadn't expected. I had to take responsibility for myself in a way I had never even thought about before.

Despite my determination, I did burnout a third (and final) time. Why? I hadn't yet learned how to manage Wanda well, and I wasn't yet willing to take complete responsibility for myself. It was hard to give up old habits and hindering beliefs because I was just plain afraid of the pictures she kept showing me. I was unsure what I would be like and how my life was going to turn out. I really did not want to accept that *I* was in charge of how I turned out, and nobody else!

Once I had Wanda under control and took complete responsibility for my actions, thoughts, and feelings (with the help of a great support network), miracles began to happen. I began attracting all kinds of wonderful people, circumstances, and opportunities into my life. I married the perfect husband, who arrived complete with an instant family. I co-created our wonderful home, and I now have a fabulous career that I love because it makes me feel really fulfilled and excited to get up each morning!

This doesn't mean that I don't have challenges. Of course I do! Every time I work on improving myself and deal with "stuff" I've created, the tide goes out just a little bit more and exposes a few more obstructions (rocks, reefs, sandbars, ocean critters) to take care of. Just as the tide continually ebbs and flows, dealing with your stuff is a lifelong journey.

The good news is that I am not asking you to deal with *all* your stuff in 30 days! I will be asking you to deal with the stuff that's got you burned out so that you can break yourself free, move on to other things, and never go back there again!

Initially, you are going to work on breaking old habits, examining beliefs that limit you, and dealing with your fears so you can get some immediate relief (space and time). Then we will move on to more fun and interesting stuff!

> **REQUEST:** Come up with five different ways to say No courteously and comfortably without lying and, preferably, without any explanation. Not giving an explanation actually reduces your stress.

Why? The difference between "Thank you, no." and "Thank you, another time." means they will approach you *another time*. You may think you are being kinder by simply deflecting their request. Unfortunately, when you do that, you set a cycle in motion that you will almost always come to regret.

The first stage of the cycle is that their timetable won't be the same as your timetable. You said "another time," meaning (at the earliest) six months from now, while they thought you meant next week.

That leads to the next inevitable stage, which is the stress from having to say *No, another time* again, and maybe again, and yet again. How many times can you say no without feeling like a total cretin?

This leads to the third inevitable stage, which is your resenting them for asking you and their resenting you for leading them on. Who wants resentful relationships? You need this? You *want* the drama? Think again!

If you *do not want another time,* don't say so! Say "Thank you, no," instead, and with a smile. It truly is kinder to both you and them and is certainly far more honest.

As you record how you spend your time this week in your Travel Log, become aware of when you say yes and when you say no. To whom or in what situations do you find yourself saying yes when you really mean no? *Why* are you saying yes? Do you need to be liked? Do you need to be busy? Are you afraid an opportunity will pass you by? Are you afraid they will get angry? Do you think they'll do something for you in return? What do you get out of saying yes? What would you get if you said no?

Identify ten situations in which you are willing to say no today and every day, starting right now. Start saying no immediately.

You will be exercising your *No* muscle and making it strong. If you need to break this into baby steps so you can build up your *No* muscle, come up with strategies that work for you. For instance, you could start with the easiest people to say no to. Might that be your family? Friends? Coworkers? What other strategies can you use?

Have a suggestion to offer whenever you say no, so the requester has an alternative solution. Chances are good that they'll remember how helpful you were instead of your "No."

Stop Volunteering
(For Now)

*Drop the idea that you are Atlas carrying the
world on your shoulders. The world would go on
even without you. Don't take yourself so seriously.*
—Norman Vincent Peale

If you are like many other people, you often inad-
vertently find yourself doing volunteer work or
being volunteered for tasks or responsibilities that,
when coupled with what is already on your plate,
only make you feel more overwhelmed.

When someone volunteers you for a task or a project at work without your consent, what do you do?
I will bet that if it's something you think will give
you greater visibility or lead to a promotion, or it
looks like it would be fun, you probably just go ahead
and take it on.

If it doesn't do any of those things, I am also willing to bet you may still not raise many objections.
You might be afraid of something (being laid off,

being thought of as incompetent, not being a team player, etc.), or perhaps this seemingly innocent, isolated request doesn't, by itself, seem like such a big deal…so you just do it.

Most of the time, though, what wears you down is not the "big" stuff, like taking on a new project. It is the "little" stuff—those ten thousand little things that are relatively unimportant and irrelevant to your work or personal responsibilities—that burns you out. You dismiss this stuff because it's usually relatively simple to do, and you figure that doing it can't really hurt. The little stuff can be things like covering for a colleague at a meeting, dropping off / picking up someone else's packages, ordering / picking up lunch for someone, making a phone call (or two or three or…) for someone else.

Please reconsider. How can doing those little things hurt you? Can you see how they could come to consume the time and space you had set aside for your own work and/or pleasure? And at what price to you? Do you see how these fulfilled requests or voluntary acts can snowball into an avalanche and take over your life?

How often do you take on little things that eat up your time and space?

A Word About Charitable / Nonprofit Work

When you give your time to charitable, philanthropic activities, you make a positive contribution to your community. In fact, when you are burned out, this sometimes feels like the only effort from which you get any satisfaction at all.

There's nothing wrong with that. In fact, it is quite wonderful...if you can afford it. By *afford it,* I mean that you have an abundance of space, time, and energy *to spare* for the volunteer work in addition to your regular work and what you need to do to care for yourself.

How much additional space, time, and energy do you truly have available?

> **REQUEST:** Stop volunteering for anything. This includes everything from picking up someone else's mail or dry-cleaning to going to a meeting for someone, and it also includes whatever activities you are doing for your favorite charity. Stop it right now.

If someone else has volunteered you without your permission, "un-volunteer" yourself immediately. (This can be tricky at work, especially if it's your boss who has done the volunteering.) Speak to that person privately, and let them know that a) you are unable to do it, and b) you want to be *asked* to volunteer in the future.

If you choose to go ahead and volunteer for something, do so *only* if you have removed enough other items from your calendar so that it does not take away time or space from anything else you are scheduled to do. This may mean giving a project away, delaying one or more projects significantly, or dropping projects completely before you take on another. If you are handing off a project, build in extra transition time before you agree to take on the new one. No working double-time!

Who have *you* volunteered for tasks without asking their permission? Whenever you have done that, how well did the person do the task? What was their attitude like? What was your relationship like?

Think of a recent situation when someone volunteered you for something without your permission. Describe the situation, how you felt about it, and what you did in your Travel Log. What didn't you do that you wanted to? Why didn't you do it?

Write down in your Travel Log three situations where you have recently volunteered someone and what the outcome was. What worked well and what didn't in each of those situations? What will you do differently in the future?

As you record how you spend your time today, note when and how much of your time went to tasks you volunteered to do or were volunteered for. For whom did you volunteer to do each task? Why? What did you get by doing that? What did you give up as a result?

Get a Buddy

*No man is wise
enough by himself.*
—Plautus

If you are feeling burned out, chances are you know at least one other person who is also feeling that way. Team up!

Working together with someone else allows you to share both the journey and your perspectives. It's easy to be so caught up in our own stuff that we overlook many of the things that are getting in our way or that could help us. Your buddy can point out these things, support you when times get a little tough, and be there to tell you the truth, even though it sometimes hurts to hear it.

Maybe you know more than one other person who's in the same spot. Invite them all to join you. The more the merrier! The more heads, the more solutions, the more support, and the more perspectives. Wow! Talk about a *super* support system.

REQUEST: Make up a list in your Travel Log of the elements you want in a buddy. Such as the kind of person that will help to energize, support, and calm you while giving good advice to help you gain new skills.

These can be qualities such as how you feel when you are with them (energized, excited, confident, calm, serene, accepted, loved, etc.), skills and traits they possess that would be helpful to you (good listener, good advisor, good sense of humor, truth-teller, direct/blunt communication style) and other kinds of help they can offer (talking to you at 2 a.m., telling good jokes, brainstorming ideas). Finally, you should consider whether or not you prefer them to be working in the same department or firm with you or not.

It is important that you consider carefully with whom you are going to partner, since they will become your primary support. You are going to share a very intimate journey for the next three weeks, so choose your buddy or buddies wisely.

You will be turning to them for insight, advice, and guidance when you get stuck on something, when you are frustrated, when you need help to figure out a new solution or to help you see situations differently. You will need them, too, when you feel down or confused and just need someone to talk you through your pain. Most of all, you'll want someone with whom to share your successes, your wins, your breakthroughs! Only someone who is burned out or has broken free can truly share your pain and anguish, as well as the *joy* when you succeed!

Identify up to five people who meet your criteria. Go ask at least one of them to be your buddy. Explain what you are doing and why. Ask that person if he or she would like to join you in the process or simply support you. If you decide to invite more than one person and create a whole group to work together, fantastic! The more people you have working together with you, the sooner you will break free from burnout!

A successful support relationship is based on *trust.* Trust occurs when there is open, clear, and honest communication coupled with doing what you say you are going to do. Should either/any of you be uncomfortable telling each other the truth compassionately, even at the risk of hurting each other, or feel that others are not "walking their talk," then the trust that you need for a successful relationship will never develop properly.

I encourage you to choose your buddy(ies) wisely and to encourage forthright communication between/among you. Give each other permission to discuss what may not be working for either/any of you and to call it quits if you cannot resolve problems satisfactorily.

Agree on how often you will communicate with each other (each day, every Tuesday, when the need strikes) and how (email, phone, support meetings). Note those agreements and with whom you have made them in your Travel Log.

> NOTE: If one reason that you feel so burned out is that you have little or no privacy in your life, and you would rather go it alone, by all means do so if it is *less stressful* for you. There are many of us who live/work in tight communities where everybody knows everyone else's business. In that case, you could choose not to have a buddy, or you could join one of the Break Free from Burnout coaching teams (see *Resources*) where people from all over the world discuss their successes and their challenges and support each other anonymously.

The choice is yours—do whatever works *best* for you.

Under-Promise, Over-Deliver

The Law of Win/Win says, "Let's not do it your way or my way; let's do it the best way."
—Greg Anderson

You want to do your work well and to succeed at what you do. In many cases, this means working faster and more furiously for a variety of reasons—"to exceed customer expectations" and "to beat the competition to market" are the two most common reasons I hear.

How many times have you rushed something only to have to redo it? How many times have you promised something sooner than you know it's truly possible to deliver?

How well does all this over-promising and under-delivering work for you? Pretty lousy, I'll bet, especially if it happens often.

When it does happen, all you do is give Wanda another shot at kicking your butt, not to mention giving all the people who were counting on that commitment you made a shot at your butt, too.

I have coached hundreds of people over the years regarding this apparent compulsion to make promises their bodies cannot keep. This behavior can stem from dozens of different triggers or origins that you could try to discover, but what really matters is that you *knock it off immediately.*

When you promise something and then do not deliver it, all you do is make a lot of people angry and hurt yourself in the long run. Sure, you may get a lot of strokes in the short term for seemingly having saved the day when you made the promise, but you will always be the first person to get kicked where it hurts the most when you do not come through.

What price are you willing to pay for being a momentary hero?

> **REQUEST:** From now on, when you are asked for a commitment, you will under-promise and over-deliver. This means you will promise less than what is asked (fewer features, a later due-date, a different component, a bigger budget, etc.) and you will then deliver more than what is expected (more features, an earlier shipping date, a better component, coming in under budget, etc.).

When you take the time to clarify objectives,

identify available resources and constraints, build in a healthy buffer on top of solid estimates, and get everyone to agree to those objectives up front, you have a win/win situation that the people involved don't have to kill themselves trying to achieve!

Negotiate extra time into the schedule, a reduction in the number of product features, a less expensive but equivalent-quality part; add 20% to your budget, etc. Then figure out how to deliver more, *reasonably*. By *reasonably*, I mean to deliver more *without* being heroic.

For example, if you can add more features to the product without sending anyone into overtime, *fantastic!* If you can find another vendor to deliver the same quality part for a lower price, *fabulous!* If you can ship the product earlier than expected, *marvelous!*

That's under-promising and over-delivering.

Reexamine any projects or tasks currently underway. **Pick three of them, and see where you can make adjustments to under-promise** (e.g., establish a new deadline). Make sure you really *under*-promise to give yourself a good margin for error! If you can manage it, then over-deliver (i.e., beat the deadline)—if and *only if* you can do so with *no stress whatsoever*. Otherwise, simply meet the new promise.

Record in your Travel Log which projects, what adjustments you will make and what commitments you will make. What differences did you notice once you switched to under promising and over delivering?

This is going to take guts. It's going to take standing your ground despite whatever level of pressure may come from another part of your company, from your family, etc.

If you *do not* under-promise and over-deliver from now on, what will you have to look forward to for the rest of your life? Higher and higher expectations that your body can't meet.

If you *do* under-promise and over-deliver, imagine what your life will be like.... You'll have breathing room, fun, satisfaction in a job well done—the exhilaration and thrill of feeling successful!

Which do you prefer?

Picture Freedom

> *Go confidently in the direction*
> *of your dreams. Live the life*
> *you've imagined.*
> —Henry David Thoreau

Y ou've just spent the past week capturing, on paper and in your mind, the ways you currently spend your time. Now that you have a clear picture of that, it's time to create a *new picture* of what you want your life to be like when you finally break free from burnout. After all, you *will* have a new life, you know. When you have a new picture in mind, one that is compelling and exciting, it will draw you to it the way a warm fire beckons you when it's cold outside. The net result is that the steps you need to take to get there will come more easily and more naturally.

Let's get started!

What do you want your life to look, smell, taste, sound, feel like? How do you want to feel when you arrive there? Free of pain? Serene? Relaxed? Content? Energetic? Smiling so much your facial muscles hurt?

What do you want or want more (or less) of in your life? Laughter? Time to enjoy your family? Working only with really smart and fun people? Less dealing with bureaucracies? Lots of exciting challenges? Learning something new every day? Being free of debt? A clean and neat home? A great romantic partner? Happy kids? A business of your own that excites your imagination? More fun?

How would you like to describe your new life? Surrounded by the sights and scents of plants and flowers? Cooking gourmet meals? Taking a wonderful vacation every year? Teaching? Writing books? Creating sculptures? Composing music? Ballroom-dancing professionally? Taking award-winning photographs? Performing with a band? Earning a black belt in *aikido*? Raising llamas? Living in another country? Leading adventure treks? Traveling around the world? Climbing the tallest mountains on each continent? Speaking five languages? Leading a non-profit organization? Running for public office? Researching a breakthrough in medicine? Negotiating world peace?

Open the jail cell you've been in, and let your heart and imagination wander free. What would your new life look like if it inspired you to wake up excited and happy each morning, in breathless anticipation of a wonderful new day?

> **REQUEST:** Review your Travel Log and the personal time chart you have created.

What have you discovered?

How do you feel about what you see there? What pattern do you see? Are you spending time the way you truly want to? Where do you have space and where don't you have space? What categories are missing that you really *want* to see there? What do you *want* to change about how you spend your time? How do you *want* your week to look?

Today, pick a time for your Sacred Hour when you have high energy, your mind is clear, and you can feel relaxed. If you are finding it difficult to relax, spend about five minutes doing some deep breathing with your eyes and mouth closed. The key to relaxing is to focus on your breath as you inhale. Feel it flow as it passes through your nostrils and into your lower lungs, then into the middle and upper lungs. Feel your belly and chest expand (in that order) as you inhale, pause, and then reverse and contract on the exhale.

Eliminate any distractions—phone, TV, anything that could take your attention away from the task at hand. If you have kids, ask a friend or relative or a neighbor to look after them for an hour, or hire someone if you need to.

When you're very relaxed, begin to create your new reality. Both in your mind and with physical representations, capture all the thoughts, feelings, textures, sounds, scents, and tastes of what you want in your new life. It's okay if you don't have the total picture yet. You can keep adding to your life-picture or changing it as you begin to see more clearly what you want your life to be like.

For now, what is most important is to capture what you want your life to *feel* like when you are finally free from burnout. You can continue to fill in more details or change them each day.

For example, my picture of life-after-burnout started with clipping out magazine photos of the ocean and of rooms that represented spaciousness to me and putting them in a file folder. Then I taped them and sprigs of lavender, rosemary, peppermint, and jasmine onto my expanding life-picture on to this huge piece of butcher paper I pinned to the wall in my bedroom. I pasted in photos of smiles, printed jokes, and cartoons that made me laugh. I wrote in snippets of songs that touched my heart.

Over a period of weeks, I created a life-picture of a beautiful, serene sanctuary near the ocean, filled with light and surrounded by a beautiful oriental garden. This was my home. I had a soulmate who was supporting my dream and loving me just as I am. I felt peaceful, joyful, excited, loved, and fulfilled.

I decided I would work from my home, and on my wall picture I created a delightful workspace where I was doing only the work I enjoyed doing. Although I didn't yet know exactly what that was, I didn't allow not knowing to bother me. I simply surrendered to my feelings and trusted that I would figure it out.

In my mental life picture, I was surrounded by people whom I respected and admired and with whom I could be myself (even if that was acting silly sometimes). I could hear lots of laughter. I knew that I was touching hundreds of lives each day. I sensed that I was bringing love and light to others. To make it more real to me, I drew stick figures of these people and labeled each of them with what they represented to me and brought into my life.

Take time to begin creating your new life today by starting to put together a physical representation of your life-picture. When you are satisfied with what you've done, think about where you can keep it so it will be very accessible so you can continue to modify it. If it's in a form that can be hung up easily, hang it in a place where you're likely to look often.

Now come up with a short phrase that will be a

theme for you. It doesn't have to be logical, impressive, or worthy of an award. It just has to mean something to you—provide something that makes your new life so real that it leaps out at you, inspires you, puts a big smile on your face, maybe even makes you whistle or hum as you go through your day. My phrase was *Joy!* Perhaps yours is *Breaking out of jail!* or *Freedom!* or *Dare to be different!* Have fun with this!

Make some signs with the phrase on it. Put the signs on the inside of your front door or bedroom door, on your bathroom mirror, your alarm clock, your refrigerator, your steering wheel, your computer monitor—-wherever you can see them easily and safely during the day so you can remind yourself constantly where you are headed!

Loosen the Reins

> *It is amazing how much people*
> *can get done if they do not worry*
> *about who gets the credit.*
> —Sandra Swinney

All too often, I've coached managers who tell me, "It takes too much time to show someone how to do this; it's just easier if I do it myself." Even if you're not a manager by profession, there may be others in your life whose time and tasks you monitor or supervise to some extent (such as your children or volunteers).

Delegating is an important skill to learn how to do well, appropriately, and responsibly and to know when to use. For managers, *not* delegating tasks actually steals from your company and limits your career. Why? Because you are paid to exercise your greatest talents, abilities, and knowledge in the most cost-effective way for the company.

For example, why should your firm pay you $100 an hour to do a task that someone who earns $50 an hour (or $20 an hour) can learn to do just as well? What if it does cost the company eight hours of your time up front to train someone else? In the long run, the firm now has another competent person to take on such tasks in the future, freeing you to focus on more challenging and strategic tasks that *only you can do* and that add value to your firm.

Face it, the higher up the management chain you are, the *more* you must delegate well or the *less* effective and valuable you become to the company. Senior management looks for this skill, and if they don't see you doing it well, you don't make the grade. You become a liability instead of an asset because they don't view you as a strategic thinker. First and foremost, good strategy is about deploying resources effectively and efficiently. Delegation is the most tangible demonstration of this skill.

I can hear the excuses now (yes, excuses!): "I can do it better myself. I can't trust anyone else to do it as well. I don't have time to teach anyone. It's faster if I do it. Nobody here is competent enough." *Yeah, yeah, yeah.* Baloney.

You need to let go of the reins. You need to delegate and then get back to the really important aspects of your work, or the chances are good that you will *not* advance in your career, and you will be buried in paperwork, working ridiculous hours and losing staff because they know you don't trust them. Talk about heading for burnout!

All of what I've said applies equally to any management task—whether you have a managerial job; or you're just starting up a business and finally realizing you need to hire someone to help you; or you're a parent trying to figure out how to balance a household budget, handle the kids' needs, and coordinate their timetables with yours.

Delegating Effectively

Think of a time when someone delegated a task or a project to you, and you were successful in completing it. Now think of a time when you weren't successful. What was the difference?

If you were successful, and the outcome was good, the following elements were probably at work:

- the task or project was well within your skill set or, better yet, an exciting and slightly big reach for you;
- you knew specifically what had to be done and by when;
- you had the time and space to accomplish it;
- you had the other resources (budget, tools, materials, help, etc.) you needed;
- you had somewhere or someone to go to with questions;
- the "how" of the task was left up to you;
- your boss checked in with you at the right times

to put you on the right track, remove obstacles, and encourage you; *and*
- you were given complete credit for the work you did.

If it went poorly, it is likely that many of these elements, if not all, were missing. (If you were successful despite that, I want you to think about the cost to yourself and/or your firm in terms of lost time, redone work, rush charges, etc., as well as your physical and emotional well-being.)

That's the difference between delegation and abandonment. Keep this in mind when you delegate, and provide the necessary elements.

If you don't delegate, you don't give people a chance to grow, and they will become unhappy and dissatisfied with their job. The top five reasons why people leave their jobs are the following:

- They are underutilized.
- They aren't learning.
- They aren't given increasing amounts of responsibility as they master new skills.
- Their supervisors treat them poorly or unfairly, do not acknowledge their work, or leave them flailing.
- Their physical work environment is mediocre or worse.

Not because they didn't get paid enough!

Did you get that? *Money* is *not* the issue. *Satisfaction and pride* gained from *growing* is!

If you don't delegate well, the net result will be that you yourself won't have the space to grow because you'll be too busy doing stuff you already mastered long ago. That mistake can stifle your career. It can also lead to boredom. Most of all, it can lead to more burnout and an even *smaller* jail cell.

So, get over it! Loosen those reins and give everybody, including yourself, room to grow, space to breathe, and opportunities to earn trust and build confidence! Your team will be more productive, and you'll be amazed at the positive difference in upper management's perceptions of your abilities.

> **REQUEST:** Delegate more effectively. This means looking at tasks that you can pass on to someone else. This applies to your home work as well.

Here's a six-step process for delegating effectively.

- *ANALYZE.* Go through you calendar and To Do lists, and identify ten tasks that it would be more cost-effective and smarter to delegate to someone else. For managers, these can be things like tracking the department budget, filling out your expense report, faxing, photocopying, screening voice-mail and phone calls, answering e-mails, creating new processes, doing research projects, etc. This request applies not only to your place of business or employment, but your home, too.

- *ASSIGN.* Seek out someone who has a skill set that could reasonably be used in each task and who is *enthusiastic* about it. If it's a task that's a stretch of someone's current abilities, you're giving them a chance to grow and demonstrate some responsibility. Don't be afraid if the person doesn't seem perfect for it. After all, you didn't know and couldn't do absolutely everything on the first day you started as a manager either. At home, such delegates could include house cleaners, gardeners, pool cleaners, window washers, children, and even spouses!

  Be prepared to negotiate some of the tasks currently on your delegate's plate so that both of you are set up to succeed. Jointly reprioritize all tasks, and agree on new deadlines, resources, etc.

- *DEFINE. Invest your time* to prepare the other person to complete the task or project *successfully.* Agree on your respective roles and responsibilities, and tell them what they are to get done and by when, what tools and other resources they can access (money, people, information sources, etc.), any constraints, what kind of communication you want to receive and how often (status reports, one-on-one meetings, etc.).

Be certain they are set up so well with the resources and information they need that the task or project doesn't come back to bite you.

- *MONITOR.* Follow their progress, and provide appropriate direction, support, coaching, and encouragement. When they have *demonstrated* competence and confidence, you will not need to check in so often.

- *PRAISE.* Most important of all, acknowledge their good work, publicly and appropriately. By appropriately, I mean that you need to be sensitive to what kind of praise they respond to best. Not everybody likes a big fuss made over them in a huge meeting with all eyes trained on them. Sometimes a simple, heartfelt *thank you,* spoken in front of the whole team, works wonders. Find out what works for *them* (not you), and do it!

- *FOLLOW UP.* Check with your people on a regular basis to see if you're delegating the way they want and need you to. Ask questions such as, "How can I help you better? What do you need from me that you're not getting right now? What could I do better to help you do [fill in task or project]. What approach might I use that would work better for you? Where or with what do you most need help? Am I delegating tasks to you that are too difficult or too easy? What other types of responsibilities would you like to take on? What is the best way to delegate something to you?"

Within the next two days, delegate all of the ten asks you identified, following the process outlined above. Mark an appointment time on your calendar to check with each delegate about their willingness, enthusiasm, and availability. Set appointments for training. Mark follow-up times to check in with them. Also set appointed times on your calendar to review your lists of tasks in the future to see if any can be delegated.

Record in your Travel Log today the ten tasks you delegated, to whom, and why. After you have delegated them, record how you felt as you did it, and note what you feel now that those items are off your plate.

No More "To Do" Lists

> *Do or not do.*
> *There is no try.*
> —Yoda

The problem with To Do lists is that they continually grow longer and longer as more items are added than are completed. Often the net result is that you feel overwhelmed and unsuccessful because you don't see any progress.

I believe that it's an excellent idea to capture a thought on paper so that it is no longer taking up space in your mind. I will be asking you to go about this a little differently than you may already be doing, so you will feel like you're making progress instead of feeling guilty, miserable, or overwhelmed.

I used to keep about ten different lists, each one labeled and dated. Of course I would lose one, so I'd start another, and I'd keep adding things. I would scratch things down on little Post-it notes and then forget to add them to the list.

Every so often I would find an original list that I'd

misplaced, and then I would combine the two lists I now had into a new third one, only to discover that the new list was three times as long as the first two because I had also found some Post-it notes and added them. I would read my lists and then beat myself up over what I had not done. Then I would feel guilty and would complete one or two items, scratch a couple off, and eliminate a few because it was too late to do them by then anyway. Then I would proceed to add five more things, so the cycle would continue.... Sound familiar?

If the way you manage your To Do's works well for you, then move on to the next chapter. On the other hand, if you feel the slightest twinge of overwhelm, failure, guilt, remorse, anxiety, or worry over all the things you need to do, then do this activity and see what results you get. If you don't have any To Do lists but need to figure out a way to handle all the unfinished stuff in your life, try this request, too.

> **REQUEST:** Get out all your To Do lists, however many there are (or create one if you don't have one already). Separate the larger projects and the individual tasks into two different lists. Include all items, whether they are work-related or personal.

Now break down the projects into their component

individual tasks, and add these to the Individual Tasks list. Next, prioritize all the individual tasks, and then make a note next to each one as to how much time that task will probably take to complete plus a good margin for error (remember to *under*-promise).

Review your Individual Tasks list. If any task has been on your list for longer than three months, put it on yet a third list, labeled "Old Tasks." (Don't include recurring events such as paying your bills.)

Get out your calendar (Palm Pilot, DayTimer, etc.). Schedule each of your Individual Tasks on your calendar, based on the priority you assigned it.

From now on, you no longer have a To Do list. Either your calendar has room for a new task or you may not commit to it.

Look over your Old Tasks. Would *not* doing any of them cause you significant harm? If they would, schedule them on your calendar, and take care of them. Such unavoidable tasks include filing your income taxes, paying your property taxes, getting a physical exam, claiming an inheritance, etc.

Toss everything left over into the trash. If you have not done any of those other old tasks by now, you really do not want to do them, you probably will not ever do them, and all *they* are doing is creating anxiety and guilt and draining your energy. Don't worry about them; if they really are important, they will reappear.

If you do not take care of an individual task at the

time when you have it scheduled, you may only reschedule it once. Move it more than once, and it goes into the trash to be forgotten. Why? Because you obviously really do not want to do it, or it's just not important enough to you to take care of it.

Stop taking on stuff you will not do. It is simply more stuff for Wanda to beat you up about. Don't give her any ammunition!

Tame Technology

Life is a grindstone. But whether it grinds us down or polishes us up depends on us.
—L. Thomas Holdcroft

Technology has gifted us with being able to complete thousands of tasks more quickly and easily, presumably driven by the intention of freeing us to have easier lives.

Really?

Then why is it that you are a slave to your e-mail, your cell phone, your voicemail, your cordless phone, your pager, your PDA, your laptop, etc., and you never seem to have a moment to breathe, pee, or be alone with your thoughts?

We are slaves as long as we allow the tools of technology to drive our behavior.

I put off getting a cell phone for the longest time, until my boss finally insisted that I have one, since it was important that sales staff and others be able to get in touch with me. I kept forgetting to fill out the paperwork or go to the store to pick it up until finally my boss's secretary did everything, and it magically appeared on my desk. (Can you tell how much I wanted this device?)

At first I was seduced by how easy it was for me to let someone with whom I had an appointment know that I was stuck in traffic, or to call my staff and remind them to do something. (Any guesses just how much they loved *that?*) Then people began to get my number, and that damnable thing began to ring all the time: in meetings, when I was in the bathroom or out shopping, during dinner....

I learned to hate it. It rang in the morning; it rang at night and on weekends. I even had three backup batteries ready at all times—one in my car, one at home, and one at work.

It became an intruder.

The last straw fell when my husband had taken me out for a romantic dinner, and the thing started to ring. He grabbed it from me, turned it off, and told me he didn't want it on in the house or when I was with him.

When he first turned it off, I panicked. What if my boss couldn't reach me? Would I get in trouble? Then, as the weekend progressed without it, I felt such a sense of relief. All of a sudden I realized that I had control again. I didn't get fired. I did tick off a few people, including my boss, but they got over it when I made it clear that nights and weekends were mine.

I began to shut off the phone when I was in meetings; then I got braver and turned it off at lunch and when I needed some quiet time to think or work in my office. I was amazed at how much more productive and effective I became once I tamed the cell-phone beast.

How much does technology rule your life?

You are still in control. You can turn it off whenever you want to. That's the key: *whenever you want to.* Who said that whenever the phone rings you have to answer it immediately? Do you really have to check your e-mail day and night and answer everyone within minutes?

We have created technologies that reinforce and push us ever further into an addictive need for instant gratification, all in the name of finding and keeping customers and delivering great service. In fact, the line between work time and personal time has now blurred so completely that we have virtually no free time and no privacy.

I am all for taking care of customers properly, but I am against it when it usurps personal, private space beyond what is healthy for us. Being addicted to technology, being a slave to it, can be as unhealthy as smoking or taking drugs.

REQUEST: Limit your exposure to and use of technology.

Install Caller ID on all the phones you can, so you can screen your calls.

Answer your work phone only an hour each day. If you make your living on the phone, take a break every hour or so, rest your ears, and do something different for 10-15 minutes.

Do not answer your (cell) phone/pager during meal times...period.

Do not answer your (cell) phone/pager once you have left work for the day, unless it is a personal call/page you are expecting.

Do not answer any phone *at all* after a predetermined hour each night or before a predetermined time in the morning. In fact, try turning off the ringer on your phone!

Make sure you have at minimum a ten-hour period every night when you will not answer, or preferably even hear, the phone.

Schedule one entire day each weekend when you will not answer your phone at all, and see what difference it makes.

Answer your e-mail for only one hour each day. If you earn your living via e-mail, take a break from the screen once an hour, and do something different for 10-15 minutes.

If you are an Internet surfer/junkie, limit such activities to one hour a day in total.

Limit how much TV you watch. TV can empty

your brain and keep you from connecting with other human beings. Starting today, limit your TV viewing to no more than thirty minutes each day. If going cold-turkey is too much for you, cut your time in half each day until you are down to thirty minutes.

Remove every piece of electronic equipment from your bedroom (phone, TV, stereo, etc.). Your bedroom needs to be a sanctuary. All those electronic devices emit electrical signals which, while they meet various safety standards, are subtly pervasive and can interfere with your sleep. Replace your alarm clock with something that doesn't startle you awake, such as a Zen tonal clock or the type that uses increasingly bright light to awaken you.

Note down in your Travel Log which actions you will take from now on. Record the differences you notice as you tame all the technologies in your life.

Clear Your Space

*Space and light and order. Those are
the things that men need just as much
as they need bread or a place to sleep.*
—Le Corbusier

If you are like most people, you have tons of stuff eating up your energy—things that just nag at you and bug you—but you feel so tired that the thought of doing anything about any of this stuff just makes you cringe.

There were times when I would let my car go for months without washing it or cleaning the interior because I simply did not have the energy; yet I hated looking at my car, was embarrassed by it, and would never let anyone see me driving it, let alone drive a client anywhere. I burned more energy skulking about in parking lots and lying about my car being in the shop than if I had just taken care of it. I was wearing myself out with unproductive excuses.

All of us tolerate a lot of things that keep us from being at our best. We have put up with them for so long that they've become a sort of mental leaky faucet.

What is wasting your energy? An uncomfortable bed? Unpaid bills? A noisy refrigerator? A malfunctioning vacuum cleaner? Piles of unread periodicals? An argument with a friend? A toothache? An overgrown garden? A long-overdue physical? A lousy haircut? Loans? Legal issues? Late tax returns? Unfinished business with an old lover? Unfiled expense reports? Untreated allergies? Grudges? Dead plants? A messy house? A leaky roof? A closet so packed with stuff that you don't dare open it?

REQUEST: Write down a list of thirty things that are wasting your energy or time or cramping your space in your Travel Log. Schedule time in your calendar to *eliminate all of them over the next two weeks.*

As they go, notice the difference in your energy level, and record that in your Travel Log. If you are like most people, the more you eliminate, the more energy, time, and space you have, and the more relief you begin to feel.

Start out with the easy ones and work up to the hard ones so you build momentum and gather more energy. For those recurring activities such as the laundry, paying bills, and washing your car, think about how you can get them taken care of automatically or more easily? Yes, we're back to delegating again, or automating.

Hire a bookkeeper, accountant, housekeeper, gardener, dog walker. Get a virtual assistant or hand-held personal organizer. Automate your bill paying with on-line or telephone banking. Hire the local garbage company to bring over a mini-dumpster, and dance as you fling away all your old stuff! Donate to Goodwill or The Salvation Army. Cancel your magazine subscriptions. Have a garage sale. Hire a local scout troop to clean up your yard or your windows or wash your car.

Meeting Mania

Hurry is the mark of a weak mind,
dispatch of a strong one
—Charles Caleb Colton

Meetings consume an enormous amount of the average workday for many people. Most of my clients who are burned out spend fifty percent or more of their days in meetings. They complain that they are stuck working late each night because they are unable to get any of their own work done during the day.

When I ask my clients if the meetings are productive, the answer is generally no. Why do you think that is the case?

For one thing, "meeting mania" has become an accepted way of doing business, one that is strongly encouraged, especially in company cultures that favor a collaborative environment. Collaborative environments are great...when they are well managed. However, when meetings take over people's daily work calendars, such environments are out of control and create more problems than they solve.

Another reason meetings are often unproductive is that instead of being used to make critical business decisions, they've become forums for people to posture, lobby, and/or socialize. The third reason is that meetings are often poorly designed and run. Not much seems to get accomplished, so no one is inspired to attend them. It's no wonder that many people practically have to be dragged into yet another meeting!

Have you ever been to a meeting that you felt great about attending and that you left with a sense of accomplishment, inspiration, direction, and/or purpose? You probably have, but the occurrence is so rare that it may be difficult to remember.

Effective meetings typically:

- last less than 20 minutes
- start on time (whether everyone is there or not—people learn to be on time when this happens consistently)
- have a clear, published agenda with just one decision to make
- include only parties who have the power to make the decision (i.e. commit resources)
- begin with those parties already having received and become conversant with all the information necessary to make the decision
- have one person leading the meeting and keeping it on task and on time
- end on time

The most productive meetings I've ever attended were held in rooms that had no chairs or desks. Talk about short, sweet, and to the point...! After all, who wants to stand around for very long?

Today, with technology to help us (web conferencing, video conferencing, telephone bridge-lines, instant chat / messenger software, etc.), meetings can happen with global participation at a fraction of what they used to cost in time and money. The temptation is there to abuse the technology instead of using it wisely.

To reduce the number of meetings you attend also means making the ones that *you call* more effective. People will want to come to your meetings because you won't waste their time, they'll make progress, and they'll feel a sense of accomplishment.

When that begins to happen, they will (un)consciously copy what you do. It will take time for this new behavior to catch on and spread, but once it does, it will spread like wildfire!

REQUEST: Set an example for others with the way you organize your own meetings. Review your upcoming scheduled meetings and make the necessary adjustments to carry out your meetings as follows:

- Schedule them for twenty minutes or less.

- Publish a clear agenda; i.e., state what decision needs to be made.
- Invite only people who can commit resources to implement the decision. No more bringing along subordinates so they "can get filled in." That's not your job; that's an attendee's job. Include decision makers **only**.
- Make sure that each attendee has received the necessary information/facts and is conversant with them.
- Make attendees aware that the decision will be made at that meeting, and get a commitment from them that they will be prepared to make that decision.
- Start the meeting on time.
- As the first item on the agenda, determine whether everyone is prepared to make the decision.
- If they are not prepared, either cancel and reschedule the meeting, or forge ahead and make the decision anyway within the time allotted.
- End the meeting on time.
- Thank everyone for their participation.

When you are asked to attend someone else's meeting, take a leadership stance and insist on a published agenda that includes the one decision to make, who will be there, the necessary information, how long it will be, etc. Commit only to those meetings that meet your criteria. Be sure to thank the leader of the meeting for running and managing the meeting so well. A little praise goes a long way!

NOTE: I am not telling you to not go to your boss's three-day offsite. You need to use your common sense. I am asking you to control what you are able to control (your own meetings) and use influence when you do not have control.

DAY 15

Choose Your "Juice"

Guard well your spare moments. They are like uncut diamonds. Discard them and their value will never be known. Improve them and they will become the brightest gems in a useful life.
—Ralph Waldo Emerson

Ever felt so tired at the end of a day that you thought you could sleep for a month? And then...wham...you find your second "wind"?

Where did that second "wind" come from? Could it have come from the unexpected letter from an old friend that arrived? Or the friend you haven't seen in awhile who called? Or perhaps it was the beautiful sunset you noticed from your car window driving home?

These examples of energy you tapped into so effortlessly, are healthy, easily renewable energy sources—pleasure, love, beauty.

If, on the other hand, your second "wind" arrived because you got a call from your boss about a problem at work or an emergency call from your parents about one of them being rushed to the hospital—that's adrenaline kicking in. And while adrenaline is a natural chemical created by your body to respond to fight or flight, aka "stressful", situations, you end up paying a tremendous price for abusing your adrenal gland.

Adrenaline is not endlessly renewable. There comes a point when the adrenal glands can begin to STOP producing adrenaline when you need it. And, in some extremely severe cases, the adrenal gland never recovers its normal functionality.

You abuse your adrenal gland when you come to depend upon adrenaline as your primary energy source. How do you know if you're doing that? Here are some questions to ask yourself:

Do you usually wait until the last minute to get things done?

Do you over-promise and find yourself scrambling to make the commitment?

Do you over-commit yourself and find you've got two parties to go to, or two meetings, or two appointments...or more?

Are you always late?

Do you create complicated solutions to simple problems?

Do you set up your calendar so you have back-to-back appointments all day long?

Are you always pointing out the direst things that can happen during a project, make it happen and then find a way at the last minute to save the day?

Do you set tight deadlines with no room for error?

Do you tend to have more problems in your life (or so it seems) than other people?

Do you set earlier deadlines than are truly doable?

Do you find yourself looking for problems and then making them into a big deal?

Do you find yourself exaggerating the seriousness of a "problem"?

Do you tailgate, speed, and/or get crazy when you're stuck in traffic?

Are you living on the edge financially, with no clearly defined way to get ahead?

Do you find yourself picking fights, often for no logical reason?

When you wake up in the morning, is the first thing you need a cup of coffee to get you going?

As the day goes on, do you find you need more caffeine to keep you going?

In the late afternoon are you searching for that candy bar, Coke, bag of chips—anything to boost you up so you can finish out the day?

When you get really tense do you find yourself looking for something to eat, drink, or inhale to take the edge off or reduce your jitters?

When you get home at night are you so wired mentally that you find it hard to fall asleep, so you have a cocktail or a glass of wine or beer to relax?

"Whoa! Wait a minute!" you say. "I do my best work under pressure."

I don't doubt that you probably do. Adrenaline is indeed a wonder drug. That is not the issue. You need to choose whether or not you're willing to pay the very high price tag that comes with abusing your body.

What I want for you is to be able to choose your "juice", not to be addicted or dependent upon it. If you're burned out, you are probably very addicted to adrenaline and using other expensive energy sources (sugar, caffeine, alcohol, drugs, nicotine) to supplement it and even out its effects. Worst of all, should you continue this addiction, you can severely harm yourself.

Wouldn't you rather rely on healthy, clean, inexpensive and effortlessly renewable "juices" such as pleasure, love, beauty, passion, etc.? Wouldn't you rather be in a position to choose when adrenaline may very well be the best energy choice rather than have it choose you?

One of the things you're beginning to experience as you break free from burnout is the reduction of adrenaline going into your system. This is a good thing, although it may not necessarily be a pleasant or comfortable thing in the short term.

Adrenaline is as powerful a drug as nicotine and as dangerous. Adrenaline addiction is condoned, encouraged and rewarded by our society. It is tied up in the American dream, the Puritan work ethic, which imply what it takes to become successful.

You have been societally conditioned to accept that becoming burned out is the price you have to pay to be successful.

There is no bigger line of baloney.

It's not true.

Fighting that conditioning won't be easy intellectually, emotionally, or physically. Especially since Wanda will be right in there telling you what a failure you will be if you don't do what she says.

So be prepared for the headaches, the coming down off the adrenaline high, the malaise, the lethargy, the melancholy you may feel. You may be lucky and feel none of these. You may experience one or more. Everyone responds differently to the reduction of adrenaline in their system.

Be prepared for people to challenge you, question you, get angry at you, because as you come off the adrenaline and adopt new behaviors, you're going to change.

You'll change because you'll begin to see other opportunities for yourself. You'll start to want a different way of living. You'll have a new perspective on things. All of that means the people around you will no longer be able to predict how you will respond. When that happens, people may no longer want to hang out with you, they'll be confused and upset.

The good news is that you will begin to attract people who are more like you and who value the things you are coming to realize that you value. So all those people freaking out and getting angry at you will soon be replaced by people of a different calibre and quality that is more suited to who you are becoming.

You _can_ do this. You've already begun the process.

Hang in there. It will get better.

> **REQUEST:** Eliminate as much caffeine, sugar, and alcohol as possible from your diet under the supervision of your doctor. I know this isn't going to be easy, but the sooner you get started, the healthier you will be and feel. Work with your doctor to figure out strategies that are suited to the current state of your health.

You will very likely be able to enjoy all these things in moderation (unless you discover you are addicted to alcohol or drugs) AFTER you have come down off adrenaline and are no longer dependent upon these substances to adjust your energy levels up or down in response to your adrenaline highs and lows.

Create two self-care habits you will do just for yourself and start doing them every single day. These habits must give you pleasure. If they aren't fun, if they aren't pleasurable, then pick something else that is and do it.

These habits are solely for your benefit. You will schedule them on your calendar. You will allow nothing to interfere with them. They are sacred.

Here are some examples:

- daily massage
- walking in a beautiful place
- reading a book for pleasure, not work
- practicing yoga or tai-chi
- working out
- going to the driving range and hitting a bucket of balls
- sketching
- writing
- meditating
- playing an instrument/joining a band
- listening to music
- dancing
- singing/joining a choral group
- play on a sports team (softball, basketball, tennis, etc.)
- gardening

Record what you choose in your Travel Log and keep track of how often you do them. If you don't do them daily, and it's possible for you to do that, what's keeping you from doing them?

Focus

As the gardener, by severe pruning, forces the sap of the tree into one or two vigorous limbs, so should you stop off your miscellaneous activity and concentrate your force on one or a few points
—Ralph Waldo Emerson

It doesn't seem to matter how big or small a company is, the most common complaint I hear from the employees who are feeling frustrated, distressed, and overwhelmed goes something like this: "Why can't this company ever focus? We rush and rush and are told to do more with less, so we do—but nothing ever gets taken off our plates, and half of the time we never get to finish a project. Why isn't anybody in management held accountable? When will we ever get to feel successful?"

Conversely, what I hear from management is something like this: "Why do I have such high employee turnover? Why can't I find qualified labor? Why do the employees waste so much time yakking in the halls? Why do employees always complain about the lack of clear direction? Why are customers so unhappy? Why are we spending money on all these programs when nothing seems to work? Why do we lose our customers? Why are we constantly chasing new accounts to make our revenue numbers? Why are expenses so high?"

If the truth be told, when I'm called in to consult with these companies, most of them are trying to be all things to all customers or clients in all markets. That's only okay if you have no competition, demand is high, and your systems are working perfectly.

Anybody you know in a position like that?

In any pursuit or relationship, the name of the game is to focus your resources to obtain maximum results. Lose focus, and you waste your resources. Money is a renewable resource; time and energy aren't. Once expended, they can't be reused or recaptured.

What, then, is a better way?

Let me offer an enduring example.

During the glory years of ancient Rome, the Roman army was invincible. Why? Because they chose a specific and achievable goal (such as conquering Gaul). Even the way they chose their goals was brilliant.

How did they succeed so well? First, they picked only countries or territories that, once conquered, would welcome the technological and cultural advantages they could acquire by being a part of the

Roman Empire: superior roads, plumbing (aqueducts, irrigation systems), productive agriculture, medical care, education, art, music. Then they brought a substantial percentage of their resources (men, materiel) to the front. They moved forward only as far and as fast as they could secure their supply lines behind them.

Once they conquered an area and could count on supplies, they left behind an engineering and law-enforcement organization to rebuild what was destroyed and to ensure compliance with Roman law. That way, each successive achievement was secured as they moved forward to the next.

One goal, three simple strategies.

The simplicity of their focus, the strategic and tactical execution of world domination, made Rome invincible for centuries.

Kind of hard to argue with that level of success, don't you think?

Behold the magic of the number *three*.

> **REQUEST:** Starting today, I want you to choose the three goals that will have the biggest impact in your professional or personal life. The first goal is to be achievable within thirty days, the second within three months and the last within one year.

Once you have decided on those three important

goals, identify the *three* most effective, impactful *strategies* per goal.

Once you have your strategies, ascertain the *three* most effective, impactful *tactics* per strategy.

Call your plan *The Magic Three* and put it in your Travel Log.

Spend 80% of your resources (people, money, time, tools, and the like) on the Magic Three.

You can change goals. You can change strategies. You can change tactics. (In fact, you will update The Magic Three every month as you focus on the next month, the next three months, and so forth.)

You simply can't have more than *three* of each of them at any time. Period.

So choose carefully. You have one day to decide.

When you focus on the three goals that will make the most significant impact—when you bring all your resources to bear on those goals—surprise, surprise! Incredible results start to happen, and fast!

Suddenly you (and your employees) have an easy method for sorting through choices and opportunities, which makes you more nimble, more competitive, and stronger.

No longer are you bogged down in endless meetings, wasting precious time and money. Mistakes are fewer. Your direction is clear. No one needs lengthy explanations. No one needs to be convinced and then convinced over and over again. Energy abounds. Enthusiasm soars. Passion is rampant.

Why? You feel successful. You feel a sense of accomplishment. You have pride. You see your direct impact. You take responsibility and like it (and so do your employees)!

All this focus translates into clients and customers having a superior experience doing business with you and/or your firm.

Customers and clients become happy. They become loyal and more reluctant to switch. They do more business with you and refer new business. This means *more profit* because relationships and resources are not being thrown away.

That's the power of *focus* (remember ancient Rome!). That's *The Magic of Three*!

Make Your Week
Work *For* You

The pessimist complains about the wind.
The optimist expects it to change.
The leader adjusts the sails.
—John Maxwell

Take some time to look at how effectively you make each week work for you. How do you plan out each day? How do you decide what you will do on Tuesday as opposed to what you will do on Friday?

I want you to think of a day when you were highly productive, when you felt an enormous sense of accomplishment, when the day passed by so swiftly that you were unaware of the time until the day was over.

What did you do that day?

Now think of a day when you felt that all you did was waste your time—when the day flew by as if out of control, and every time you looked at the clock you freaked out because you didn't have much time left to get anything done.

What was the difference between the two days?

On the day you didn't get much done, you may at first have felt exhilarated from working at top speed and juggling so much at once, but then felt empty at the end of the day because you felt that you had gotten nowhere.

Odds are good that on the day you got a lot accomplished, you were focused like a laser beam.

When you *focus your resources* (your thoughts, energy, time, space, etc.) and bring them to bear *on one objective* (for example, increasing revenue by a certain amount by June), with *one strategy* (creating a new widget to solve the thingamajig problem for digital musical composers) on *one tactic* (writing the design specifications or locating the best source for a particular component), you can't help but make incredible progress and move forward quickly.

When you spread your resources across multiple objectives, strategies, and tactics, you can move forward over a broader area of achievement, but much more slowly and unevenly.

REQUEST: Reorganize how you handle your work week in order to make it more effective.

Yesterday you figured out where you were going to put 80% of your resources. In today's activity, we're going to deal with the resource of *time*.

Eighty percent of a five-day work week is four days. So you will devote four days of the week to achieving your three goals, using three strategies per goal and three tactics per strategy.

Of those four days, I want you to select three— one for each of those goals. Label each day by the name of its goal. Let's say that Monday is Goal One, Tuesday is Goal Two, and Thursday is Goal Three.

On your *goal days,* you do only activities that lead directly to achieving your three most important goals. These are activities that only you can do and that yield the biggest bang for the time spent. For example, if you were the owner of an advertising agency, your most impactful activities would probably be meeting with potential customers, deepening relationships with your most profitable customers, and working on long-term projects such as developing new technologies and methodologies for increasing advertising and communications effectiveness.

I want you set aside the fourth day as a *support day* to handle all the administrative and follow-up work you generated on the previous three days. In our example, let's call Wednesday Support Day.

On the fifth day, that we will call Maintenance Day, put aside *one hour* for daydreaming. I'm serious—*daydreaming.* This is your time to shut your eyes or stare out the window at something beautiful and just be quiet: no phones, no e-mails, no pages, no interruptions, no reading books, no *nothing*. This is your creative time. This is time to let your mind wander and your intuition roam freely. It is amazing what ideas, solutions, and feelings will surface because you've provided a space for them to appear. (This is a good time to doodle in your Travel Log.)

The remainder of the day can be used as the twenty percent of your time that's available to do the stuff that just "comes with the job." This could be your day to meet individually with your staff, file your expense reports, catch up with your network, attend a seminar, or give a presentation

Days Six and Seven are Play Days. You need time to decompress from work. You need time to have a life. You need time to explore who you are—to recapture your playfulness and nurture yourself and your personal relationships. So…this means no work-related activities of any kind—phone, e-mail, voicemail, reading any business material (reports, periodicals, etc.). I want you to spend *a minimum of eight hours each weekend* doing *only* what you really *want to do*.

Note in your Travel Log how you have decided to structure your week. How does it feel to have a structure for your week? What differences do you notice in yourself and others? How is it working for you?

DAY 18

Stop Chasing Perfection

A pint can't hold a quart—if it holds a pint it is doing all that can be expected of it.
—Margaretta W. Deland

How many times have you labored to make something perfect, only to realize that the only person who noticed or cared was you?

How many times has Wanda beat you up because what you did simply wasn't "perfect" enough?

How many times have you said to yourself, "Why should I bother doing this? I won't get it right anyway" or "Nobody will appreciate it anyhow"?

These are examples of a perfectionist's thoughts. What feelings do these ideas bring to mind? Struggle? Pain? Discouragement? Defeat? Inadequacy? Anger? Frustration? Self-pity?

Do you feel them? Does someone you know feel them? Are *you* chasing perfection? Do you *want* to keep chasing it? Webster's New Collegiate Dictionary defines perfectionism as "the doctrine that the perfection of moral character constitutes man's highest good; the theological doctrine that a state of freedom from sin is attainable on earth; a disposition to regard anything short of perfection as unacceptable."

I am not here to discuss the first two. It's the last definition I'm interested in because it is the one that traps most of us. Why we've trapped ourselves isn't important. What is important is recognizing that we've *chosen* to believe this idea, and it's especially important to realize that *we can choose to believe something else!*

How has chasing perfection helped you? How has it hurt you? Is it still hurting you?

When I was younger, chasing perfection pushed me to achieve remarkable accomplishments. Because I believed so strongly in doing everything perfectly, I graduated from high school a year early and at the top of my class. I graduated from college a year early so I could go out and "make my fortune." I received extraordinary promotions and held unimaginable positions of responsibility for my age and experience in my workplace. I got my MBA by attending school full time while also working full time. This striving for perfection helped me to become the best that I could be, no matter what I took on...and no matter the cost; and it did serve me for a time.

Somewhere along the way, as I got older, I began to realize what a toll this belief was taking on my life. It was no longer serving me very well. The more successful I became in corporate life, the harder it was to be "perfect" all the time.

I became afraid to make mistakes because I felt that people were penalized for making mistakes at work. I became hesitant to take on new challenges because I feared that I might not do them perfectly. I got angrier and angrier with my staff, my peers, and partners who didn't do their work perfectly. I felt sorry for myself and frustrated because I had no control over anyone else's performance. Ultimately, I stopped learning. When you stop learning, you stop advancing, you stop growing, and you die. I "died" at 36 when I burned out for the second time.

At thirty-six, I was not a very pleasant person. I was a bundle of anger, hostility, and cynicism. Then one day after talking with my best friend (who was brave enough to tell me what a witch I had become), I finally accepted that my constant striving for perfection was wreaking havoc in my life.

Can you relate to the good and the bad results of striving for perfection? Each of us has our own story, our own pain, and our own journey. Many of us have reached the other side. If you have, I want to acknowledge you for that achievement! That was a tough lesson. For those of us who still struggle with our Wandas constantly telling us that what we do is never good enough...I'd like to ask you a question:

Have you ever experienced a perfect moment in

time? Almost everyone has. Think back and find that moment—a moment when it seemed as though time slowed down so radically that you were able to be completely aware of every detail. Perhaps you heard the rustling sound of leaves in the breeze, felt individual blades of grass, noticed a loved one's delicate eyelashes and smelled the scent of their skin, glimpsed the pain in a someone's eyes or the fading color of a dying flower, felt the harshness of a cold wind. *Perfect* can be beautiful or ugly; it can be joyful or sorrowful.

What was your perfect moment in time? What was it like? How did you feel? Would you like to experience such moments more often? Wouldn't you enjoy feeling "perfect," just as you enjoyed these "perfect" moments?

You can.

YOU are perfect right now.
YOU are enough right now, just as you are.
YOU are a magnificent masterpiece in progress.

And you will become even more aware of your perfection every day as you learn, grow, experiment, explore, make mistakes, teach, share, correct course, accept, receive, love, give, evolve. Are you willing to shift your thoughts and feelings so that ***perfection is a journey, not a destination***?

Perfection *is* a journey, *not* a destination! On this journey, you can *choose* to experience perfection every moment along the way.

Doesn't that sound and feel a lot more compelling than struggling to reach the top of a mountain taller than Mount Everest and feeling like you'll never get there...and then once you actually get there, feeling exhilarated for awhile, only to feel exhausted at the thought of climbing the next mountain?

Pursue Perfection Only if It Gives You Pleasure

Pursuing perfection can be healthy or unhealthy, depending upon the reasons for doing it. An *aikido* master takes pleasure and satisfaction from his continuous work to learn and perfect each movement, each motion, and his inner sense of calm. Although he may never achieve "perfection," he is in a continual state of "perfecting."

While painting "The Last Supper," a perfect work of art, Leonardo Da Vinci said, "I am still learning."

Monet was fascinated by the play of light on his environment. He sometimes set up five or six canvases next to each other so he could capture the perfection of the light as it gradually cast various levels of shadow throughout the day.

Someone who seeks perfection for the pure pleasure and joy of it, for the deep sense of fulfillment that comes from the pursuit of it, understands that perfection is a pleasurable experience to be felt along the way, not simply a destination to be reached. In such circumstances, then and only then does the pursuit of perfection become a healthy energy source and not a debilitating one.

If this is you, fantastic! Go for it! Be sure this process of perfecting feeds your soul. If it drains you, brings you more anguish than pleasure, reconsider whether the pursuit of perfection is right for you or will simply continue to contribute to burning you out.

> **REQUEST:** Examine your daily actions to see where you might be chasing perfection (perhaps without even realizing that's what you are doing).

How does pursuing perfection help you? ("I turn out high quality work all the time. People can rely on my word completely, so they trust me.")

How is it hurting you? ("I spend hours perfecting something, and I am never fully compensated or appreciated for the work I do. I have to fight constantly to make sure we do everything right, and it seems like I never have an easy day at work.")

To what degree does the pursuit of perfection make you more miserable than filled with pleasure and joy?

Note in your Travel Log all your thoughts and insights about how pursuing or chasing perfection helps or hurts you.

Accept that everybody around you is doing the very best they can. Few people set out with the deliberate intention to do a lousy job. Demonstrate your acceptance in the following ways:

Calmly and respectfully ask, "What was your intention when you did (not do) such-and-such?" Use exactly those words—no more, no less—whenever you think they don't care enough, did a less-than-perfect job, or deliberately screwed up, or when you think they are getting in the way of your doing a great job. Be open to their answers. Listen to them, and do not react immediately. You just might be surprised at the answers you get.

Acknowledge the people around you whenever they do anything right, no matter how small. Do it every time, starting *right now*. This statement needs to be truthful, said sincerely and with a smile on your lips and in your eyes. Look them *directly in the eye* when you say it. If you don't really mean what you say, people will know it, and your credibility will be tarnished.

Here are some examples of acknowledging statements:

"Bill, I really appreciate the way you organized that report. You made it so easy to read."

"Sue, thank you for taking the time to be so thorough."

"Jim, you really made the people in the meeting feel at ease."

"Joan, the customers really enjoyed your presentation."

"Tony, your weeding in the garden perked it right up."

"Ellen, you cleaned the floors so well, I could practically eat off of them."

Why do I want you to do all this?

I am asking you to trust me enough to do these things without any explanation, and see what your experience is and what you learn by doing them *every day*. Keep an open mind as you do these activities over the coming weeks. Note what works for you, and do more of it! Discover what does not work for you so well, and experiment until you find what does.

Use your Travel Log to capture your thoughts and ideas, feelings and impressions as you readjust your approach to perfection.

Choose Your Attitude

The "as if" principle works. Act "as if" you were not afraid and you will become courageous, "as if" you could and you'll find you can. Act "as if" you like a person and you'll find a friendship.
—Norman Vincent Peale

Every day we wake up and decide, usually unconsciously, what kind of day we are going to have. We do this by way of the attitude we adopt. What kind of attitude might that be? Grumpy, reluctant, or tired? Cheerful, enthusiastic, or energetic?

Attitude is a choice. It is a *choice* we make, regardless of the weather or other external events and regardless of the state of our physical condition. Since attitude is a choice that we make, it is under *our control*, and we *can choose* to be and feel whatever way we want, whenever we want.

Sound farfetched?

Many years ago, I managed a group of telemarketers. As I analyzed the way the group functioned, I was initially stymied because two of my ten TMs always had exceedingly high customer-satisfaction ratings, day after day and month after month. They consistently out-performed everyone else. I began to observe them closely and noticed several exclusive elements of their behavior.

Both were always upbeat. They were always polite (even when a customer was screaming at them on the phone). They were generous and kind to their colleagues, sharing tips and secrets and helping the others. This behavior was consistent despite the fact that one of them lived with and cared for a parent who was dying of cancer and the other was a single parent, living from hand to mouth.

I finally asked Ruth and Bill, "How is it that you can maintain your cool and enjoy your work every day?" Their answers were phrases such as, "I want to have a great day, so I make it great for me." "I want to enjoy my life every day, and life's too short to spend it being miserable."

At that moment, I realized that *attitude is a choice.* They woke up every day choosing to feel positive and happy because it gave them the energy to enjoy their day. An attitude was not an act or a mask that they put on. Once they chose an attitude, they actually felt it.

In *choosing* to be happy, Bill might say to his mom, "Gee, Mom, it's a gorgeous day outside. Shall I put you by the window so you can watch the garden?" and his attitude brought a smile to her face and joy to their hearts. By choosing to be cheerful, Ruth could handle the latest kiddie crisis (missing shoes or homework, hurt feelings) with equanimity and enjoy her children instead of being frustrated by them. When Ruth and Bill arrived at work, their attitudes energized them so well that they always had a successful day.

How about you? What attitudes do you choose unconsciously or out of habit?

REQUEST: When you wake up in the morning, notice what you're feeling. Name it. Will this attitude be the most effective for you today, or might another attitude serve you better? What might you choose to embody? Enthusiasm? Cheerfulness? Optimism? Persistence? Determination?

Whatever it is that you choose, close your eyes and recall a time when you had that attitude in the past. Remember how various parts of your body felt then. What did your arms feel like? Your back? Your neck? Your eyes? Your mouth? Your stomach? Your legs? Your throat? How did you move?

Got that? Okay, now stay there for a few moments, breath deeply, and remember that this is how you want to feel *all day* today. Make a gesture with your hand that you will remember easily. For example, tug your ear, grab your elbow, make a fist. Do this five or six times so you create a "body memory" you can easily recall just by making that gesture.

Whenever you get caught up in the day and begin to lose that feeling, make the same hand gesture, breathe deeply, and remember again how your body felt. Let your body settle into that feeling; then do something to reinforce your attitude.

What might be one thing you can do today that will continually reinforce your chosen attitude? Smile at everyone you see? Let the phone ring three times before you answer, so you can take a deep breath and relax? Say a sincere "thank you" each time someone does something for you? Whatever it is—*do it!*

Note down in your Travel Log how you felt during this experiment. What was easy? What was difficult? How did people react to you? How did you feel? What was your day like? How was it different from days when you did not consciously choose a productive attitude and then make sure to sustain it?

Eliminate Your Energy Vampires

We need to find the courage to say
NO to the things and people that are not
serving us if we want to rediscover ourselves
and live our lives with authenticity.
—Barbara De Angelis

Energy vampires are people who virtually suck the energy out of us. These people aren't always easy to identify because we have become so accustomed to them that we do not realize what they are doing to us.

Many of these people are completely unconscious of their behavior. They do not necessarily intend to be so negative or emotionally draining. Despite their good intentions, we still need to limit our exposure to them, or they will drag us down with them.

Here are some clues to help you identify the vampires in your life:

- They can be sarcastic, cynical, bored, and boring.
- They make jokes at others' expense.
- They gossip and put other people down.

- They complain and whine continually.
- They say they want what's best for you when what they really mean is that they want what's best for themselves.
- They're the first to blame someone else for their mistakes and the first to take credit for others' work.
- They're closed-minded, inflexible, unkind, demeaning, and even cruel or mean.

Most often, vampires are very needy people, wanting more from you than you are able to give comfortably. They may also want more *of* you and can be quite jealous, possessive, and resentful if they have to share you.

Here are some typical situations involving energy vampires:

A coworker stops by your office/cube and proceeds to whine, complain, and make cynical and sarcastic remarks about the company, his boss, his job, the management—you name it. He goes on and on while you listen, but all you can think about is finishing your report, and you wish this guy would just shut up and go away. *How much did you really enjoy his company?*

A friend calls and invites you out to dinner. You agree, but at the last minute, she cancels. *This is the fourth time she's done this to you.* How many more times will you let her hurt and inconvenience you and renege on her commitments?

A client calls and says he needs a product sent to him overnight. It's closing time, but you stay late and get it done. The next day, he calls and complains that the shipping was too expensive. Do you *want* clients like this?

A friend is getting divorced. She's obsessed with how much she hates her ex-husband and can't stop talking about it, no matter where she is or with whom. You, on the other hand, have just started a new relationship with a wonderful man. You are filled with love and excitement. She's resentful of your happiness and constantly tells you that your relationship will end, too, because all men are awful. How *inspiring* do you find her?

Your brother calls and asks to borrow some tools. He says he'll return them next weekend. The next weekend, then the *next month,* comes and goes, and he still hasn't returned the tools. No surprise there; he's done this before. When you finally ask him, he says, "What tools?" Do you *enjoy* replacing your tools?

I remember a time when I was guilty of being an energy vampire. I was in my early twenties, working in the publishing industry. During the first six months that I worked at one particular job, I became friendly with a woman who had the office next to me. One day, she asked if she could speak with me privately, invited me into her office, and closed the door. She proceeded to say that she no longer wished to speak with me unless I had something positive to say. She told me that I was "tainting her day" with negative comments, and it was difficult for her to do her job with any joy or pleasure when I was constantly complaining about someone or something.

Wow! Talk about feeling humiliated! My face was red and burning, and I slunk back into my office and shut the door for the rest of the day.

At first I was angry. *Who was she to say such a thing to me?!* All my defenses went into motion, and I just avoided her. I wouldn't even say hello to her anymore; I would just nod my head curtly. I thought that depriving her of my company was punishment. (Is that arrogance, or what?!)

Shortly after this incident, I noticed how much happier and how much more productive she was. She was soon promoted. In the meantime, I continued to be negative, whining and blaming until I was let go.

The message was repeated when I invited another woman from my company to lunch with me and a contact of mine who worked at a well-known broadcasting firm in New York. As we were walking back to the office after the lunch, my coworker told me that she appreciated the introduction but that I had thoroughly embarrassed her by speaking poorly of the company where we worked. As a result, she no longer wanted to associate with me, since she felt I had been so unprofessional.

Wham! More humiliation; yet I still could not hear the message clearly. In fact, I did not understand the message until some fifteen years later when a whole series of similar incidents began happening to me *daily*. Talk about crisis mode!

I will forever honor the people who had the courage to deliver these messages to me, even when I could not hear them. The messages were the same and were always in response to my habitual whining and blaming and playing the victim. The most powerful message of them all, which was also the hardest to hear, was to have the courage and self-love to surround myself with healthy, energy-exchanging relationships. It is a message I will not soon forget.

If you are still having trouble identifying your energy vampires, here are some questions to ask yourself:

- Do I truly look forward to spending time with them?
- When I am with them, do we create positive energy together?
- How do I feel after I have been with them?
- Do they treat me respectfully (honor my time, feelings, needs, requests)?
- What do I get from being with them?
- Do they play a more positive or a more negative role in my life?

- Would I want to be stranded on a desert island with them?
- Do we bring out the best or the worst in each other?
- Do they encourage my growth?
- Do we grow together?
- Are they excited and sincerely happy for me when I succeed?

How would your life be different without these vampires in it?

REQUEST: Might you be an energy vampire? Could you be guilty of depleting energy from others?

Give some thought during your sacred hour today as to whether or not you seek out people to suck energy from. Record any feelings, thoughts, or observations about this in your Travel Log.

Also in your Travel Log, identify 10 people who suck your energy away and with whom you come into contact at least once a month.

Immediately reduce the amount of time and frequency you spend with these people.

To reduce contact, here are some suggested strategies:
- If you see them once a month, make it once every three months.

- If you see them once a week, make it once every four weeks.
- If every time you see them it is for a dinner, make it a twenty-minute phone call instead.

Next to each person's name in your Travel Log, make a note as to how often you've seen them or spoken with them up until now, and for how long, and how much time (if any) you will spend or how often you will speak with them from now on.

Take a look at your calendar, and determine whether you have any activities planned with any of these people. Take immediate steps to bring those activities in line with what you have outlined.

Reduce, reduce, reduce your exposure to their negativity!

Is this going to be easy? With some of the folks you identify, yes; it will be easy because you will recognize just how draining these people are, and it will be a relief to reduce or eliminate the time you spend with them. With other people, especially those you are close with emotionally (whether family or friends), it may be disconcerting, even hurtful to realize that they are draining you.

You may find that, in order to become healthy and to flourish, you will need to remove some of these people from your life, if only temporarily. That may scare you because you have become accustomed to being around them. They have been filling a void in your life.

Nature abhors a vacuum. I want you to imagine that if you create this void, this vacuum in your life by getting rid of your energy vampires, wonderful people can now come into your life to fill that space!

As you go through this process of reducing your exposure to energy-depleting people and stressful elements, make notes in your Travel Log about how you are feeling and what you are discovering.

Upgrade Your Community

Every man is like the company
he is wont to keep.
—Euripides

You have begun to reduce your exposure to the people in your life that are draining you. As you do that, you are creating a void, a space for other people to take their places—people who can open your eyes, open doors, present new opportunities, expand your universe, help you to rediscover yourself or to become someone new.

Why is creating that space important?

When you are burned out, you have a tendency to hang around with other burned-out people or with people who continue to burn you out. As crazy as your life may seem at times, you are stuck in a rut, a routine. Being surrounded by these people is like being stuck in a limited "situational gene pool." Eventually your situations and perspectives become so inbred that you lose the ability to identify differing perspectives and new opportunities, and you remain stuck in burnout.

New people can present new pictures and new soundtracks with which you can experiment and, if they feel right, adapt for yourself. Imagine if, instead of being surrounded by the people who are in your life now, you could have access to and spend time with people who inspire you, who fire your imagination, who are incredibly creative, who have integrity, who are fun, and so forth. Imagine having just the right people around you to help you grow and achieve what you most desire....

Just as your Burnout Buddy is helping you to break free, a whole new community, people who are *not* burned out *and* who are fully alive and engaged in their lives, can accelerate your personal development simply by your being around them. If you could tap into the perfect community for you, who could you become? What could you do? In fact, *what could you **not** do?*

One day when I was deep in the throes of burnout, feeling sorry for myself and angry at the world, I went home to find that my boyfriend had brought some friends to my house to party and watch football. After having spent the entire previous weekend cleaning the house to a level of detail I rarely ever did because I had so little energy, I had left it sparkling clean. Now, I walked in and discovered that the house had virtually been destroyed. The kitchen was a complete shambles: there was food on the floor and counters; dishes were all over the place; the gas stove rings were coated and just disgusting. I won't even go into what the rest of the house looked like.

I lost it. I was livid with anger. The depth of my fury was enormous, but what was truly amazing was that it was directed at *me*, not them. At that moment I realized fully that I had allowed myself to be surrounded by people who wasted my time and energy. They were drunk (many of them were alcoholics), they were stoned (it was my boyfriend who was supplying the marijuana), and I HATED IT.

I realized how low I had sunk. I never used drugs, I didn't even like the taste of alcohol, and yet the people all around me did nothing more than work at the easiest jobs they could find so that they could make just enough money to get loaded and party every chance they could get.

I threw them all out...including my boyfriend. I ended our relationship right then and there and never looked back. I had finally realized that the company I was keeping *kept me where I was*, and I *hated* where I was. I didn't have a plan for what to do next; I simply knew that the kind of people I wanted around me were not in my living room that night.

The next day I began contacting all the people I had been longing to spend time with—people who were brilliant, talented, passionate about what they did, extremely witty and creative, and excited about life. I began to surround myself with the type of people

I *aspired* to be and, in doing so, I began to rediscover lost parts of myself and to reinvent myself. I didn't really plan it; I reacted out of instinct. I was actually *starving* for the right people to come into my life.

Don't wait years to create a community that nurtures and inspires you. DO IT NOW!

> **REQUEST:** During your sacred hour today, allow your mind to roam. Remember the situations you have been in and all the different people you have met or seen or spent time with who have inspired you, touched your heart, struck a chord, made you tingle with excitement and anticipation, aroused your passions (no, this is not a sexuality exercise!), made you smile, supplied you with energy, spurred your imagination, or filled you with gratitude, joy, and a sense of peace.

In your Travel Log today:
- Capture your thoughts and feelings about who these people are and what they are like. What is it they offer you that you want more of?
- Are they smart, funny, self-assured, well-traveled, intellectual, financially stable, compassionate, creative, curious?
- Are they painters, musicians, computer geniuses, successful investors, brilliant business owners, happily married couples, poets, dancers, metaphysics

buffs, classic movie fans, outdoor-sports enthusiasts?

- List the places where these various people hang out, anywhere in the world. What types of magazines do they read? To what organizations do they belong? Where do they go and what do they do on vacation?

- List people you know personally who fit your list. Begin to spend more time with them. Invite them over for dinner or to an activity you would all enjoy.

- List people you know who could possibly know someone who would fit on your list. (Networking experts say you are only four people away from the person you need. The larger your network, the more chances you have to find who you are looking for.) Ask for introductions to these people, and meet them.

- List activities these people participate in, such as business trade shows, outdoor adventure treks, metaphysical retreats, bookstore lectures, and the like. Pick three activities taking place over the next three months that are within your budget, and *go to them.*

- Show *interest* in these people. Spend time getting to know them and what makes them tick. Learn from them, and share what you know.
Consider yourself from their point of view:

- Who would these people joyously welcome into their lives? Would it be someone who is open, curious, comfortable taking financial risks, self-confident, physically fit, calm, accepting, demanding, a great listener, relaxed, challenging, imaginative, a good audience, a person of integrity, free of self-deception, humble, gracious?

- What changes if any, do you see making in yourself to be compatible with such people? Are these changes you are excited about making?

Use your Travel Log as if it were a canvas to "paint" a picture of your perfect community and what kinds of things you do together.

Over time, you will begin to grow and expand your community beyond where it is today. It will evolve as you begin to discover what really interests you and with whom you have a healthy exchange of energy. This evolution takes time and it takes space; it may also take effort to put yourself out there because you'll probably feel awkward and uncomfortable, especially in the beginning. This feeling will pass with time as you learn and refine the list of people to invite into your world and the reasons why. Eventually it will become effortless.

You will make mistakes; you will get hurt from time to time. All of that is part of the process of learning and growing along your journey. Go easy on yourself (and if you stumble, look for the lesson).

Become a No-Gossip Zone

Speak ill of no man, but speak all the good you know of everybody.
—Benjamin Franklin

Gossiping—speaking ill of, or with intent to harm, anyone who is not in your presence—is a way of keeping distance between yourself and the person with whom you are speaking.

It is so much "safer" to keep our walls up with chitchat, isn't it? Getting to know someone else means allowing them to get to know you, and that can make people feel very, very vulnerable.

Vulnerable, yes—not defenseless. You don't have to be defenseless. Being defenseless means laying yourself bare and susceptible to attack without discretion or good judgment. Being vulnerable means choosing which parts of yourself you will lay open, when, to whom, and under what circumstances.

Gossip is a major cause of misunderstanding and a form of deliberate cruelty, and it has the potential to backfire on you in many ways. Even when phrased in politically correct terms, a malicious statement will come back to haunt you when you least expect it. I know of more careers and friendships that have been blown to bits because of gossip.

I want you to think for a minute about a time when you have needed to confide in someone. What criteria did you use to choose that person? Whenever you ruled someone out, what was the reason? Oh...a habit of talking about others? Hmmm....

I will never forget one incident when someone betrayed my trust through gossip. I was consulting with a firm, and I had confided in someone who worked there that I was going to have to make a decision about continuing to work with the company. My reasons had to do with the firm's policies and the way I felt they violated my personal and professional ethics. I had not resolved this dilemma in my own mind and was still working it out. I had elicited this woman's thoughts about the company's policies and her ideas on a potential resolution.

A few days later, this woman went out with some other people from work, including the CEO, to whom I reported directly. She got drunk and proceeded to tell him about my situation. The next day, the CEO called me to his office and demanded to know what was going on, whether I was planning to leave, etc. He accused me of blackmailing him into changing the company's policy simply to satisfy my own standards, with which he did not agree. He accused me of setting up the whole situation so that he would find out from another source. He was furious and was ready to cancel my contract immediately.

I was completely blind-sided, especially as I had worked out in my own mind a way to resolve this as a win/win for us both. Thankfully, we were able to work things out (although it took several months to reestablish full trust between us). However, this particular woman held a position in which she was entrusted with a lot of sensitive information, and the CEO then felt unable to rely on her to keep confidences. It turned out that he had been debating for the previous few months whether or not to keep her on as an employee. This incident helped him make his decision, and the woman was let go shortly thereafter.

When you are burned out, there is enormous temptation to gossip because you are tired, angry, and in pain. You complain, you moan and groan, and rarely is it about something you yourself have done. It's almost always about other people and how they have let you down, done something stupid, etc., etc.

I want you to really think about the message your gossiping sends. When you speak negatively about someone who's not there to hear you, others wonder just what you are saying about them when they are not around.

Is this the message you want to give?

If you want to be viewed as trustworthy, reliable, and possessed of good judgment, cut out the gossip. Stop working at being interesting. Gossips yak for one reason—to be the center of attention.

> **REQUEST:** Become a "no-gossip zone." Do not participate. Do not encourage gossip tacitly by allowing it to go on in your presence even when you say nothing about the person(s) being discussed.

Begin to notice when and how often you talk about others who are not present. Whenever you realize that's happening, just stop. Allow your thought, or the other person's, to conclude, then steer the conversation back to a subject concerning the person you are with: "Tell me about your project. How's your job going? How's the house remodeling coming along?" Draw people out; be interested in them and what they think, feel, know, believe. Remember to be *interested*, not *interesting*.

If anyone talks about someone else who is not present, especially in an uncaring or malicious way, you can say something such as, "I'm uncomfortable talking about Bill when he's not here. Shall we ask him to join us?" Chances are good that gossiping person will not want you to include Bill and will stop talking about him.

Having said all that, there is a difference between listening to someone "vent" and gossiping. When people need to vent their emotions, it's often helpful just to listen. Neither agree nor disagree with their statements; simply provide support for their feelings. For example, you might say, "I can understand how/why you feel this way" or "I am so sorry you had this experience."

Do not get involved in judging the people being discussed or providing an opinion about them. That's gossip. Go on supporting the speakers' feelings and, eventually, when they have run out of steam, ask them what they want to do at that point. Keep talking? Change the subject? Do something else? When possible and appropriate, encourage others to take their concerns and feelings directly to the people they are discussing with you.

If people persist in wanting to know what you think about someone, tell them only *one positive, factual thing* that you have experienced *personally* ("John has been kind to me; I have observed Ann doing good work; I enjoy Jim's sense of humor."). Then redirect the conversation back to the other person's feelings or to another topic that would interest both of you.

If someone asks your opinion of another person, and the question is in regard to skill levels, such as with a job reference, stick to the facts. The facts consist of what you have personally and directly experienced or have observed about that particular person...no more, no less. Do not pass along what other people have implied or recounted to you.

Most important, treat all conversations with total confidentiality, whether you are asked to do so or not. Be especially sensitive to this issue if you are married or involved with someone in whom you typically confide. When other people speak to you in trust, that does *not* mean that they automatically extend that trust to your partner.

Do these things well and consistently, and you will earn the trust and confidence of others.

Note in your Travel Log whenever you notice yourself gossiping, what it is that you discuss, and about whom. Observe any patterns in what you say and about whom you say it. The words we speak about other people are often mirrors of what we feel about ourselves.

What, if anything, did you learn about yourself? Think about it.

Build Your Fences

*If you don't take charge of shaping
your own destiny, others will
apply their agenda to you.*
—Eric Allenbaugh

When you purchase a home on a piece of land, you are given a deed that shows the boundary lines of your property. This document is filed with the local government so you know for certain that the property you paid for belongs to you, and so does everyone else. You might also put up a fence to delineate and protect your property.

If you bought some land, would you allow your neighbors to build on your property without your permission? I doubt it. You would probably make it very clear to them that they did not have your permission and would insist that they desist (unless there was some tremendous advantage to allowing it). If a neighbor started to build a shed on your land, for example, it's likely that you would take action immediately to stop him from doing so. You'd probably do whatever it took to protect your land, from telling him to stop, to deliberately dismantling or damaging the work he did, to taking legal action. It's very unlikely that you would simply stand by and let him encroach on your property.

Given that, would you then please explain why you'd be willing to take strong action to defend your property...but are more often less than willing to take such strong action to defend your personal boundaries—boundaries you may allow to be violated day after day, week after week?

Your boundaries can be crossed in many ways. At work, such infringements might include being expected to cover for someone when that person has make a mistake, or being asked to cancel your vacation because you can't be spared from the office. Your personal boundaries can also be ignored if your relatives show up unannounced to visit for weeks at a time, if someone smokes in your car without asking permission, if your furniture is destroyed by a friend's child.

There are many ways in which you can participate in allowing others to infringe on your boundaries, such as permitting people to yell at you or verbally abuse you, allowing yourself to be bullied or intimidated into working ridiculous hours, or rushing to help someone in an emergency when it is their own lack of planning that caused it in the first place.

Why are you willing to let people treat you less respectfully than you treat them?

I am not accusing you of being a complete doormat. I *am* suggesting that if you are burned out, you are probably less than clear and consistent about where you put your boundaries and how strongly you defend them.

In 1988 I was working full-time while also attending graduate school full-time to get my MBA. I was not working for a small, easygoing company, either. My firm required employees to eat, drink, live, and breathe solely for the company in order to be accepted as a part of the family. It was a sign of honor and loyalty to say, "I worked 110 hours this week, stayed all weekend long. What did you do?" (I could gag when I remember how low my boundaries were.)

For three months, my department experienced reorganization after reorganization. When the dust settled, my boss took another job in L. A., and I got to take over her job as well as continue to do my old job, keep one employee and lose all but one full-time contractor (I'd had six), and remain at the same rate of pay.

I allowed my managers to take advantage of my need to succeed, shine, and be a hero, no matter the personal cost to me. I would complain loudly from time to time, but in the end, I would back off when I was accused of not being a team player ("...if this is more than you can handle…") or was promised a promotion or raise sometime later on (none of which materialized). I could see a recession coming, and I was afraid, so I shut up.

I had *no boundaries*. I LET THEM OWN ME.

If my boss felt like screaming at me, he did so with impunity; if the president needed a new or updated analysis, I stayed all weekend to do it; if I asked for a vacation and was told it wasn't "a good time," I canceled my trip (I had no vacation for two years).

My wake-up call came in late 1989 when my grandmother died. I had hardly seen her during the previous year when she had been so ill. I did not even speak with her very much during the last month of her life. I am embarrassed to say that I barely made it back to New York for her wake and funeral. I never got to say goodbye.

My grandmother and I had been very close, as she had brought me up while my parents were working full-time. Her death brought everything into brilliant and painful focus for me. Because I had allowed the people at my firm to violate any and every boundary, I missed out on sharing the last days and months of her life, which would have made her departure easier for us both.

REQUEST: Build your fences!

A boundary is an imaginary fence or shield that you place around yourself to protect your heart, your soul, your mind, your body, and anything else that is important to you. You put up boundaries to defend yourself from the damaging and harmful behavior of others toward you. You, and *only* you, can define where your boundaries begin and end.

When you are burned out, the odds are good that your fences need to be better constructed, more clearly defined, and extended as far as possible. Without these fences, you will continue to suffer needlessly.

You have already begun much of this work. You have been saying no and building up your No-muscle and have also limited any volunteer work. You are recognizing when you are afraid and learning to manage your fear. You are eliminating or reducing your contact with energy vampires who sap your emotional resources.

You have been putting a gag over Wanda's mouth more often.

You have reduced your exposure to technology and have eliminated wasteful meetings. You've taken care of many stressful things you have been tolerating, and you're under-promising and over-delivering.

You are now focusing your resources and making your week work *for* you, not *against* you. You are also more aware of when you are chasing perfection and how far you are willing to go to do so. You are choosing better energy sources and weaning yourself away from those that hurt you.

All of those activities were designed specifically to support you and strengthen your fence-building muscles. Now you need to go a step farther and move your fences way out to the absolutely maximum circumference of your "personal property line."

List ten things that people may no longer do to you, say to you, or do around you...ever. At all. Period. No negotiating.

These are things that debilitate you and make you feel less than who you truly are. This list includes sniping, making nasty comments, and offering destructive or negative criticism. Such affronts are no longer permitted.

Write these in your Travel Log the way you would write down a rule. "No one is permitted to yell at me" is an example. If you have more than ten, go for it! Write them all down, and don't worry about how precise they are. Just capture the gist of what you mean.

Now rewrite them so that each boundary is even bigger and stronger. For example, "No one may abuse me verbally by yelling or being rude, discourteous, disrespectful, snide, cruel, malicious, or mean." Wow! That's a much bigger boundary! Do you see how much more personal property you are protecting with this type of boundary?

Next to each boundary, list all the people who tend to violate those boundaries. That's right, list everyone, from your minister to your mother to your boss's boss.

Regarding people with whom you come into frequent contact and/or who are very important to you: Talk to each one individually, and tell them that you are finally becoming clear about your boundaries, and state how you want them to treat you from now on.

Discuss the consequences if they do not honor your boundaries, e.g., you will leave the discussion, you will no longer see/talk to them—whatever you have decided the consequence will be.

Get their commitment to respect each of the boundaries that they have previously violated.

Ask them what *their* boundaries are and if and how *you* may have violated any of them. *You must stop violating their boundaries immediately*. If you do not, then they have no reason to honor yours...do they?

They may not always know what their own boundaries are, so you may have to help them articulate their issues. Questions such as these can be of help: "Do I do or say anything that drives you crazy or upsets you? If you could make (not) doing that into a rule, what would it say?"

Regarding those people who honor your boundaries, thank them, reward them, and tell them how very much you appreciate their support.

For those people who violate your boundaries, here's a four-step process you can use:

- Tell them or reiterate what they have been doing. ("I have asked you not to abuse me verbally.")
- Ask that they stop doing it immediately. ("Please lower your voice and speak respectfully.") If they do it again...
- Demand that they stop immediately. ("Stop speaking to me this way, right now.") If they continue...
- Walk away. Leave. Remove yourself from their presence. ("I am leaving because what you are doing/saying is not acceptable to me. When you are in a calmer state, I will be happy to resolve the issue.")

This can get tricky at work, especially if it's your boss! Use your common sense. I personally would not shout *"Stop it!"* I might say, "I cannot continue this dialogue if you cannot speak in a normal tone of voice," or "I will return to speak with you when you can speak in a normal tone of voice," or "Speaking to me in a raised tone of voice is a sure way to make me defensive and unable to hear what you are saying. Please speak normally so we can have a reasonable conversation."

You are probably not going to get this right all the time. You are likely to slip and forget occasionally. Don't feel badly if that happens. It takes time for new habits, new muscles to form. Do expect that when you slip, putting your fence back in place and keeping it there may be a bit more challenging and take longer. Accept that it may take a few tries before you get the hang of this and before you have retrained the people around you.

Do not overwhelm yourself. Pick one boundary a week, and integrate it into your life.

I suffered for years by allowing myself to be caught in the middle of dramas between various family members until I made it clear that I wanted to hear about only the good stuff that went on among them. I insisted that I would no longer participate in gossip, and I would not even let them vent to me because it so distressed me. Once I did that (although I did slip from time to time), I cannot even begin to describe how much lighter I felt, how much freer my life was, how much better my relationships with each of my relatives came to be. I only wish I had done it sooner.

Setting boundaries with parents, siblings, lovers/partners and other loved ones is not the easiest thing to do, yet boundaries are necessary for your health and well-being, regardless of the relationship you may have with a particular individual.

Only you know how ready, willing, and able you are to place your boundaries where you choose and then to defend them. You are the one who will live with the results of your choices.

Clearly defined and reinforced boundaries make

the difference between being a victim and managing your life. Stop being a victim!

Take control of your life. *You can do this!*

Record in your Travel Log what you've discovered about yourself since you wrote down your boundaries and began building and defending them. What were you most afraid of? What surprises were there? What turned out to be easier than you thought?

Fortify Your Fences

Hold yourself responsible for a higher standard than anybody expects of you. Never excuse yourself.
—Henry Ward Beecher

In the last chapter, we talked about determining how you want others to treat you and establishing boundaries to protect yourself. Now it's time to talk about your personal standards of behavior, *your* code of conduct—in other words, how you choose to treat other people.

Your personal standards are a choice. You can set them at any level you want. What might that look like?

In my case, when I was younger I prided myself on telling the truth...well, telling the truth most of the time. (This is an average standard for behavior.) I was not yet able to acknowledge that white lies were still lies, regardless of their color.

I eventually came to understand that when I told the truth, regardless of any consequences, I actually had less fear and more freedom. I no longer had to worry whether someone would find out that I had somehow colored the truth, and I was able to use that freedom for doing other things.

Today I make a point of telling the truth, phrased as constructively as I know how, regardless of the consequences. (This is a much higher standard.) I am not always as successful as I want to be, but it is a standard I have set that allows me to sleep better at night and feel that I am doing the right thing for others and myself.

How does having a personal standard help with boundaries and burnout? Your boundaries are set up to protect you from others. Your standards fortify your boundaries by building them stronger and higher. When your boundaries and standards are in poor condition or are misaligned, burnout is inevitable.

Here are some examples:

When you treat people with complete, constructive honesty (a standard) all the time, how long do you think they might continue to lie to you (a boundary)?

When you take complete responsibility for your actions at all times (a standard), how long do you think people who shirk theirs and blame others will be in your life (a boundary)?

Having personal standards is not about feeling morally superior or being self-righteous. It is about creating a code of honor, a code of behavior by which you will live. When you do that, you are fully expressing *who you are*, because there is no finer expression of integrity than *actions* that match your *standards* and *boundaries*.

The higher and stronger your fences, the less junk will end up on your personal property. You won't have to expend so much energy dealing with people, things, events, and situations that hurt you or waste your time.

When you are in burnout, your fences are not in the right places, they are not maintained well, they are not always attached together, some are higher than others, and some you have even forgotten about completely. It's no wonder you feel the way you do (when you *can* feel)!

Mend your fences and fortify them, and you can become stronger, freer, less needy, and rediscover the real you!

> **REQUEST:** Mend and fortify your fences by identifying your standards and then living them.

Who are the people you most admire? What is it about them that you admire? Are they honest, open, decisive? Are they fair? Do they treat everyone kindly? Write down their attributes and actions in your Travel Log.

Your standards express who you are as a person.

What are your standards now? What are your rules for treating other people?

Write down ten of your standards in your Travel Log. If you need some ideas, use the examples of the people you admire, and determine if any of their standards inspire you so much that you want to adopt any of them for yourself.

Some examples of ways you could phrase such standards are:

- I tell the truth constructively.
- I wear my heart on my sleeve.
- I put forth my best effort, and I don't hold back.
- I do not speak poorly or unkindly of anyone.
- I treat everyone courteously.

Do these standards you have written down feel right for *you* today, as you have expressed them? Are of any of them standards you think you *should* have? Ask yourself why these particular standards are important to you. If you feel some sense of obligation or guilt toward a standard, or some difficulty in embracing it fully, let it go. Forget it. It's not for you, at least not now.

Another way to test a standard is to accept it and immediately begin living with it for twenty-four hours. Pay attention to your body and how it feels as it lives with this standard. If your body feels tense, tight, it may not be for you. Rework the language, and then live with it for an additional day.

Eventually you will know when you have articulated your standard clearly because your body will feel at ease, relaxed, and yet full of energy.

Do not set your standards higher than you can handle. The last thing you need to do is set yourself up to fail. When you are burned out, it is extremely important that you under-promise and over-deliver to *yourself*.

Do not say that you will always tell the truth if you cannot begin to live that way right now. *Do* create a standard that is reflective of what you are ready, willing, and able to do right away.

Note that the higher your standards, the stronger are your boundaries—the taller and more fortified your fences become. This means you have a well-protected space where very few things will irritate you. You can be yourself; you will no longer tolerate people, places, and things that do not honor you; and you will be able to keep out all the stuff that could drive you nuts.

As you become stronger, as you recover your personal energy and direct it better, you can set your personal standards even higher and aim for them, much as I aim to tell the truth constructively regardless of the consequences. I am not completely there yet, but I am close, and I look forward to the day when I can finally say that I do this all the time. I can feel the difference already in the progress I have made, and this inspires me to want to go even further and make that standard mine in every pore of my body.

A combination of the following elements is what will keep you from becoming burned out, now and in the future:
- putting your well-being first
- clearing your space
- creating boundaries
- setting ever-higher personal standards
- maintaining all of this behavior well

Start today, right this minute, and live by your standards.

Walk Your Talk

Do not say things.
What you are stands over you the while,
and thunders so that I cannot hear
what you say to the contrary.
—Ralph Waldo Emerson

When designing a building, an architect may refer to its structure as being "in integrity." By *integrity*, the architect means that the building's structural elements are properly integrated as a whole so that the entire edifice is sound and able to withstand the pressures of such disasters as earthquake, hurricane, flood, fire, and the like.

Just like a building, when you are in integrity—when you are whole—and a disaster strikes (such as an unexpected illness or death, a job termination, or a tax audit), you respond with less anxiety and greater composure. You remain whole instead of collapsing out of fear and panic.

There are varying degrees of integrity and wholeness, and *you* are the only one who can define what wholeness looks like and feels like to you. Being whole, being in integrity, is a *choice* just like everything else.

When you are whole, when you are acting from integrity, you have a clear conscience. A clear conscience is necessary if you want to get out of burnout and stay out. Why? Because whatever weighs on your conscience eats away at you, both consciously and unconsciously, day after day. It drains your energy and obstructs your ability to see and respond to opportunities.

Years ago there was a period of time when I habitually neglected my financial responsibilities. I paid my bills only when I felt I was up to it. It wasn't that I couldn't afford to pay. I had plenty of cash. Having money was never the issue; not paying my bills on time was! I wouldn't face how badly behind in payments I was because I just did not want to deal with it. Consequently, I felt guilty, inadequate, stupid, and ashamed that I was such a coward.

My "brilliant" solution was to make even more money. I somehow figured that if I had more money, this problem would go away. (Why I ever thought that making more money would automatically absolve me of making timely payments is still a mystery even to me.)

I worried every day and every night about how far behind I was. I was burned out, tired, emotionally exhausted, and ticked off, yet willing to spend energy getting angry whenever companies sent me late-payment notices. I was clearly getting energy from this anxiety (nice adrenaline rushes) and, at the same time, it was draining energy from me because I was wearing myself out. I was simply unwilling to find a way to pay my bills on time. I wanted someone to rescue me. Can you believe this? I lost sleep worrying instead of getting out of bed and just doing it!

Finally my CPA, who was also a dear friend, refused to do my taxes any longer because all this chaos made the job a misery for her. Talk about a wake-up call! I did not want to lose her friendship or her respect. I told her I was overwhelmed with paperwork and detail and asked for her help to figure out how to handle this chore without having to get bogged down in detail (which I loathe).

She introduced me to online banking and automatic payments. I automated all my bill paying, and since that time (more than ten years ago!) I spend no more than twenty minutes each month on whatever finance-related details I need to address.

Once I owned up to this problem and fully resolved the issue so it would never return to bite me, I felt so incredibly free, so *alive* again. I felt enormous satisfaction and pride. Guilt, shame, and embarrassment were gone. For the first time in years, my conscience was clear (in this area anyway), and I no longer lost sleep over it.

To resolve this problem, I had to embrace my irresponsibility, believe that I was completely capable of managing my finances well, find the right solution to complement my strengths and weaknesses, set a standard always to pay my bills on time *and then do it,* with no exceptions.

Now is the time for you to embrace and take full responsibility for what you choose to do and not to do. This does *not* mean that you take the *blame.* It does mean that you take care of the issue and solve it so completely and so well that it does not come up again.

This is not about ethical or moral rights and wrongs. This is about *you walking your talk.* It is about putting your boundaries and standards into more than just words or actions that are merely in your defense. It means fixing situations that you have created as a result of your actions or lack of them.

REQUEST: Act with full integrity, as you define it.

Make a list of ten different ways you are not walking your talk. Look at your boundaries; look at your standards. How well do you uphold each of them? Do they contradict or strengthen each other? Where they contradict, realign them. What are the consequences to you if your boundaries are higher than your standards? If your standards higher than your boundaries? If they are different from each other in any way?

In your Travel Log make a list of ten unresolved matters in your life that need to be taken care of. What is out of whack in terms of your boundaries and standards? What's going on in your life, as a result of either your actions or inaction that clearing it up completely would unburden your conscience?

Is there anyone you dread seeing or would feel uncomfortable meeting by chance? Is there anyone you have hurt, injured, or damaged in some way? Have you come to closure with all past relationships? Have you kept all your promises, no matter how seemingly small or trivial?

Find whatever will work for you to take care of these unresolved matters so you can have a clear conscience and live in integrity at last! Deal with all of them as quickly as you are ready and able.

Stop whining. It just keeps you where you are.

Stop blaming. It merely digs your rut deeper.

Stop agonizing over the past. You cannot change it.

Stop making excuses. Taking action is what matters.

Stop burying your head in the sand. Ignoring it won't make it go away.

Stop waiting to be rescued. "They" can't "fix" you or your problems.

You fix them so that they never happen again.

Receive Graciously

What you are comes to you.
—Ralph Waldo Emerson

If you're like many other people, you probably find it relatively easy or fun to *give*, while *receiving* is much harder, perhaps even uncomfortable at times.

Why is that?

Let us look at giving for a moment. What is so great about it? Well, you get to pick whom you are going to give something, what it is you are going to give, when you are going to give it, where you are going to give it, and how you are going to give it. Did I leave anything out? Oh, yes—you get to feel great because you made somebody happy or did something good. Nothing wrong with any of that.

So think about that for a minute...as the giver you are in complete control, aren't you? For most people, being in control means feeling safe.

No wonder we enjoy giving—it's totally on our terms!

Do you secretly, in the back of your mind, tally up how much you give? Be honest. How many times have you given to others and then, when you needed them, they did not give what you needed or expected in return? Were you hurt? Were you disappointed? Were you angry? Were you resentful? I am not saying that this is true all of the time, but I would bet it's true more often than not.

Now let us return to receiving. What makes it so hard for us to receive, whether it is a compliment, a thank you, a material gift, whatever it might be? Why is it so hard? Well...what's the opposite of being in control (giving)? *Ahhh*...being out of control and thus vulnerable. Yes, indeed, to receive means to open ourselves and be vulnerable, to give up control and accept the gift offered.

Why else is it hard? Do you wonder constantly what string is attached? In the back of your mind, do you often second-guess the giver's motives? *Oh, my!* Will you have to give back a gift as lavish or expensive...or as meaningful? What do you have to do in return? Do you deserve it? What do they really expect?

I can remember being angry with someone because I felt that this person was not giving enough to me in return for what I'd given. I felt that I had given and given and given, and I got nothing back. Now I was empty and had nothing left to give.

Duh! I had a million strings attached, and the

more I tried to bind him to me by deliberately giving more and more (and, yes, this was a former partner), the more he resented me. After all, why the heck would he want to give back to me when I demanded it! Deep in burnout, I could not see this dynamic until many years later. Needless to say, the relationship ended (for a variety of reasons—this was just one contribution) with both of us angry and resentful.

What if you could learn to receive graciously? By that I mean simply accept gifts at their face value, and say a genuine thank you with no guilt, no self-doubt, no need for reciprocity. How different would you be? How would receiving feel different to you?

Project yourself into that space—and now, how would your giving change? What would you do differently? How would giving feel different to you? Now imagine how wonderful a gift your gracious receiving could be to someone else....

REQUEST: Practice the art of receiving graciously.

Give *yourself* something wonderful, and experience the receiving of self-love, self-care. **Pick five things you can give or do for yourself each day**. You have already started some self-care activities. Add these five to them.

The next time someone gives you a gift—whether it is a compliment, something material, or something someone does for you—smile, and say a sincere thank you. Let go of any need to reciprocate, any guilt over how much money they have spent on you or how much work it may have taken on their part. Just be in the moment, and enjoy the gift. Show your pleasure sincerely to the giver.

Note in your Travel Log the feelings you get when someone gives you something and when you give to someone else. What differences do you notice, if any?

Examine your motives whenever giving. Check to see that you have no string attached, that you are not doing it out of guilt or fear or the need to tie a string.

The next time you get angry or hurt or upset when someone isn't there for you, for whatever reason, take a look at the reasons for your anger. Is it because you "gave" to them and so you expect them to "give" in return? Dig deeply into this issue. Often there are hidden beliefs governing our reactions and our behaviors. This particular topic is a big, sticky, hairy, prickly one!

What is Wanda telling you? Observe her and note in your Travel Log what she says.

Take some time to sort through these thoughts and feelings. Begin to de-clutter your belief system by rejecting what you no longer truly believe, and adopt the beliefs that are yours and yours alone.

Receiving graciously means being open and taking pleasure in the pure joy of the act.

Practice makes perfect! The better you become at receiving, the better you become at giving!

Identify Your Needs

If there is to be any peace it will come through being, not having.
—Henry Miller

Like most of us these days, you have probably flown in enough planes by now that you could recite any airline's in-flight safety recording by heart—especially the instructions "...should the oxygen masks drop down, please put your mask on first, make sure it is properly fastened, and then you may assist other passengers...."

Do you recall the reasoning behind that instruction? The logic is that there is absolutely no way you can help anyone else with a mask if you have already passed out from oxygen deprivation.

"What the heck does this have to do with burnout?" you ask. A lot.

Putting on your oxygen mask first is a wonderful example of being selfish.

Okay, I saw you twitch at that last word. I saw your eyes widen just slightly and your body go rigid for just a bit. You probably felt a slight twinge of discomfort.

Why is that? The thought of being "selfish" raises all kinds of uncomfortable feelings for many of us. The first time I thought about this, guilt came rushing at me. How did you feel?

Being selfish in a healthy way is smart and is also necessary to break through burnout successfully and never go back there again. Otherwise, you could be there a very long time.

By common definition, the word *selfish* describes your intention when you take from others, regardless of the cost to them, in an attempt to get your needs met. In our current use, however, being *selfish* means that you are actively *investing* in your body, soul, mind, heart, needs, integrity, and life.

Let me illustrate what I mean by this.

Imagine that when you were born, your life was a beautiful, clean, perfect cup. It had no chips, cracks, or stains. Your handle was the perfect size and was completely whole. Love, kindness, joy, and lots of other good things were poured into your cup, and you accepted and held it all with grace and gratitude.

As time went by, your cup became chipped; it got stained, and the handle broke off a few times. Now there are cracks galore.

Throughout your life, varying amounts of praise, understanding, esteem, security, prosperity, and the like, have been poured into your cup; yet they continually seep out, and you seem unable to hold onto them for very long. You look to others constantly to fill up your cup, and some do; but many are tired of giving to you, so they stop. As a result, you have to keep finding new cups to tap, which takes even more energy away from doing what you really want to do.

Now imagine that your cup's cracks are mended, the chips are gone, the stains removed. You are complete and content with your cup. All of a sudden, cups you have not encountered in a long time and cups you have never before encountered can see how attractive your cup is, and they begin to pour understanding, praise, esteem, security, and prosperity into your cup. In fact, your cup is now overflowing, so you start giving away the excess.

Now go back to your cracked cup. Remember when other cups asked you for praise or esteem or understanding? How did you feel about giving some to them when your cup was leaking or if it was completely empty?

Return to the image of a whole cup, overflowing with understanding, praise, and esteem. This time around, how does it feel to give understanding and praise?

What's the difference between giving from a cracked cup as opposed to a whole cup?

With a cracked cup, it is virtually impossible for

you to give anyone anything because you do not even have enough of what is in it for you. If and when you are able to give even a small amount, chances are good that you feel a little angry or resentful about doing it, though you may not always admit it. ("Not again," you say with a sigh, or "Why do they always come to me?" or "Can't they ask someone else?")

When your cup is whole, you are able to receive all the good stuff that's out there ready and waiting for you. You're in a wonderful place because you are receiving so much that, indeed, your cup runneth over, and you can give without harming yourself.

If instead you harm yourself repeatedly, over and over again, you deplete what you have to give. If you care for yourself first, however, you will always have more than enough to give away.

The cracks in your cup represent the needs you have that are not being met. They are draining away all the wonderful things you want in your life. How long and how hard are you willing to work to obtain a continuous surplus of what you want, sufficient to keep your cup full, while it's leaking all over the place?

Can you see how chasing hard after what you *want* before you get your *needs* taken care of can send you into burnout? Doing this means that *whatever you want will never be enough to make up for your unmet needs*. All that effort and adrenaline, wasted on filling a cup that cannot possibly remain full!

Our Needs Drive Us

Our needs will always drive us because if they go unmet, we cannot survive; we cannot be who we aspire to be. When our needs go unmet, we become quite unhappy and unpleasant.

For instance, I deeply need to express my creativity—a fact that I accepted fully only about a year ago. Before then, I treated it as an option. For many years I was completely unaware of this need. The net result: I drove everyone around me completely crazy when I could not express my creativity. I now express it in a variety of ways that include writing, painting, playing piano, leading retreats, and interior decorating, and even in the way I approach coaching my clients.

To me, creativity means being inventive, coming up with new and better ways of doing things. During the time when I worked for a very famous high-tech firm that was known for creativity, I was in my element. Although not always rewarded for it, we were encouraged to come up with creative solutions to really tough problems. That creative freedom partially sustained me as I was burning out. It was not enough to satisfy my need completely, but it was just enough to keep me from uncovering how important creativity was to me.

When I left that firm and went to work with yet another big, well-known high-tech firm, the freedom to express my creativity was completely shut down.

As a consequence, I told lies, betrayed confidences, derailed all kinds of projects, simply to make things happen the way I needed. Was I aware at the time that I was doing these things? Heck, no! I rationalized away my actions. I was willing to do almost anything to fulfill my unmet need.

Fortunately my boss recognized my problem and was able to create a job for me where she could best direct and harness my creativity. Although neither of us could have put it into words at the time, I can now see from a distance why I did things I would never even consider today. I behaved in ways that were thoroughly embarrassing when I realized (years later) the extent to which I'd gone in the attempt to resolve these unmet needs.

When your needs go unmet for long periods of time, this intense repression and frustration contributes to burning you out. Why? Because you are running around like a maniac, doing all kinds of things that are not fulfilling in order to make up for the fact that you do not have enough of what you need. Your suppressed needs take over and turn you into someone you don't recognize.

I am willing to bet that the person you are today is *not* the person you remember having been before burnout. I am also willing to wager that you may not particularly like yourself right now and are struggling to figure out who you really are and what you truly want.

Beware: Just like me, you will do practically any-thing and everything (and probably already have) to get your needs met! It's part of being human. Rather than demean yourself (*How could I have done that? I should never have done that!*), it's time to take action to recognize which needs are going unmet and figure out a healthy way to satiate them. You see, you *can* fulfill them completely and move on.

Once you do, guess who is in the driver's seat. *You are!*

> **REQUEST:** Become aware of your needs, and iden-tify at least five of them. A need is something you require every day in order to be at your best. It is not optional.

Today you start Phase One of handling your needs so you can stop being "needy" and move on to feeling stronger and more satisfied with your life.

Notice whenever you go into *auto-pilot mode*. By this I mean when you catch yourself automatically beginning to react or over-react to something without even thinking about it. Do not analyze it for now; just let it happen. Observe what happened before and after you reacted, and describe in your Travel Log everything you remember as soon afterward as you can. Keep your Travel Log with you so you can record the incidents as they occur. Do this for one week.

There are many types of automatic reactions: going to work in the morning and arriving without remembering how you got there, lying to someone without thinking about it, becoming impatient, losing your temper, pushing to get ahead in line, cutting someone off in traffic, giving in to your kids rather than inviting an argument (or conversely, shouting them down out of habit), pushing someone to agree with you, hogging the limelight, "one-upping" someone (their story, their accomplishment), and the like. Some of these behaviors will be relevant to this topic, and some will not. It doesn't matter; simply capture them all for now.

Look especially carefully for situations in which you suspect your behavior is *inappropriate*, and you cannot seem to control yourself.

For example, I noticed that I would automatically challenge anyone who said something such as, "We do it this way here." For me, that was like waving a red flag in front of a bull! My auto-pilot would kick in, along with an instant rush of adrenaline. I would immediately interrogate (and I do mean *interrogate*) that person in a belligerent and demeaning manner. Most times it was as though I was watching someone else do all these things, because I somehow felt that this was not "me" (at least not the "me" I thought I knew).

At the end of the week, look over your notes, and

list the need you think is causing each behavior. You may need to enlist the help of friends and coworkers to help you figure this out. As uncomfortable as this may feel, don't be afraid to dig deep here. Once you have identified these needs, you will be well on your way to breaking completely free from burnout.

Please don't avoid this. Persevere, stick with it!

There may be instances when more than one need will be listed. This is not unusual and is to be expected because we are complex creatures, and you are unique!

Here are some examples of needs: to be respected, to be treasured, to be needed, to be comfortable, to be heard, to be touched, to be calm, to accomplish, to be acknowledged, to be rewarded, to be accepted (or considered "cool"), to be free, to be clear/have clarity, to be secure, to be safe, to control, to be right, to be on guard, to do the right thing, to obey, to prove yourself, to be independent, to be self-reliant, to have order, to be organized, to be messy, to be strong, to be recognized, to be famous, to be acclaimed, to be responsible, to be busy.

Now prioritize your needs in your Travel Log.

Here are some hints for prioritizing: Does a particular need appear on your list many times? The more often it appears, the more it is pervading your life and controlling you. Also ask yourself which need, if it were completely met today, would then provide the greatest immediate benefit to you.

In your Travel Log, describe who you would be and what it would be like to be around you if this need were completely met, once and for all. How would your life be different? How would you feel?

Satisfy Your Needs

*Nothing can bring you
peace but yourself.*
—Ralph Waldo Emerson

In the previous chapter, we talked about identifying your needs. With observation, you will become more aware of them as the week goes on. Sometimes that's all it takes for you to put your finger on some of the more insistent needs you have!

With that in mind, I want to introduce you to Step Two in handling your needs—and satisfying them so well that they never return.

As a result of building and fortifying your fences (establishing your boundaries and your standards) you have already set up two systems to help get your needs met! By establishing boundaries and standards, you have addressed what you are no longer willing to accept in your life, which is one way to handle a need. For example, if you decided, "No one may abuse me in anyway," that is equivalent to insisting, "I need to be treated well." If you decided, "I will always tell the truth," you are saying in effect, "I need truth in my life."

Your fences are critical elements of your integrated structure. They provide a foundation so you can build a working system on top of them. A system? Yes, an internal system. It's sort of the way that plumbing works in a building. It's built in, and you can set it up so that it delivers or takes away water, either constantly or on demand!

I first addressed my need for creativity by remodeling my new home and then redecorating it. I also signed up for an art class. This part of my system was like being able to turn on one of several faucets when I wanted hot water. I could go out and stencil the outside of my garage, or I could attend a class.

I arranged to have home-decorating catalogs sent to me. They arrived frequently and automatically, sometimes two or three times a month! I looked forward to their arrival. I set aside two Sunday mornings each month when I could peruse them at leisure. This was like having running water constantly available because I could reach for the catalogs any time, and new ones always arrived without my having to do a thing!

What is most important to realize is that once you have satiated a need to the point that you are nearly wallowing in the excess, that specific need will most likely dissipate entirely.

In my case, I got to a point where I was drowning in catalogs, and my home remodeling project was 90% complete. I felt completely sated, and the hunger, the drive for creativity, has abated. I was able to move on and not feel diminished in any way. I canceled the catalog subscriptions and now use my Sunday mornings to putter in my garden.

> **REQUEST:** In your Travel Log, write down next to each need specifically what actions you will take, and when, to get that need fully met.

For example, let us postulate that you need to be recognized. You have realized that no matter how many awards, bonus checks, plaques, and thanks you receive, or how often you are told you are great, you still find yourself upstaging other people in meetings, grumbling or feeling jealous when someone else gets recognized, demeaning someone else's accomplishments, or taking credit for work you really did not do.

You may find yourself demanding a bigger raise, more stock options, a larger staff, a bigger budget, and then complaining that the bonus wasn't big enough or the stock options were insufficient. No matter what your boss or coworkers do, it's never enough. You always feel unappreciated and complain constantly that you aren't treated as well as some other people. Your boss and coworkers are frustrated because they cannot seem to win with you.

Facing up to what you really need and admitting the truth about it can be very painful and embarrassing. It often means looking at yourself and not being terribly pleased about what you see.

What a perfect opportunity! *Now* you can do something about those needs and finally satisfy them. Just think: You *never* have to act like an uncouth barbarian again!

Let's talk about what kind of systems you could set up so you would be recognized, fully, once and for all, and stop driving yourself and other people crazy!

In your Travel Log, describe the perfect ways to be recognized at work, home, with friends, and so forth. Would that be a sincere thank-you, offered by the president in front of the entire division? Might it be a bonus check and a handshake from your boss in private? Could it be a standing ovation?

In your Travel Log, create a table with three columns. Label them from left to right with "What I need to be recognized for doing or being," "How I wish to be recognized," and "Whom I need to recognize me."

Now fill it in. Here are some examples:

What I want recognition for doing/being	How I wish to be recognized	Whom I need to recognize me
My hard work at home and at work	Verbal thanks for doing a good job; a $1000 bonus each year from company	Coworkers, Boss, Spouse
My brilliance	Remind me of my moments of brilliance; ask for my help to solve difficult problems	Mom, Dad, Spouse
Coming in under budget	A verbal thank-you and a gift certificate to my favorite restaurant	My VP, My CFO
Creating a terrific product	Stories about how easily the product sells or how it has solved problems	Salespeople, Customers
Fixing a leaky faucet	A kiss, a hug, and a home-cooked dinner	Spouse
My jokes	Laugh loudly and ask for more	Spouse, Friends
Not striking out	Cheer me on	My Softball Team

Now ask for what you want.

If any of the people you have asked forget to do their part, just ask them whenever you need it. You will have to help them get into the habit. Remember, you are setting up a new system, and there are bound to be glitches now and then.

The more open you are about explaining *why* this is so important to you, the more *ready and willing* they will be to do it and the more often they will *remember* to do it!

Start getting your needs met today. Start with one, and then add others as you begin to feel that need become fully sated.

Describe in your Travel Log what you are learning and discovering about yourself and others as you go through this process.

It will take some time for you to put your systems in place and fix the bugs so that things are working well for you. You may get discouraged from time to time, but don't let that stop you. If you find yourself not making progress with a need, let it go and work on another for awhile. Switch back and forth as necessary in order to keep making forward progress. Eventually you will find what systems work best for you, who is helping you the most, and who is hindering you the most (the bugs), and your needs will finally be fulfilled.

Give yourself permission and plenty of room to make mistakes and, most important of all, permission and room to *succeed*! You will find that after awhile, each need will be so well met that it no longer drives you. Each crack in your cup will finally be filled! As more needs are met, more and more cracks in your cup will be filled. The system you set up repairs the cracks. The better the system, the stronger the repair. You want each crack to be fixed so well that it never opens again!

To continue with our analogy, once the cracks are filled as a result of your systems working well, all the recognition and other good things you get will begin to fill your cup so high that it finally overflows.

And once that happens...*ahhhh...!*

What does the picture of a whole cup evoke for you?

Live Simply

A man is rich in proportion to the things he can afford to let alone.
—Henry David Thoreau

Now that you've reached this page, my greatest hope is that you will have absorbed and accomplished most of what we have talked about. You are at the top of the burnout-abyss ladder, you are about to open the door of your burnout jail cell, and at this moment you are paused to step into freedom.

To take that next step means that you are finally prepared, willing, and able to simplify your life greatly. Why are you able to do this? Because at this point you are living in integrity, and you are in the process of satisfying all your needs once and for all.

The more aligned and in integrity you are, the more your needs are met and the fewer your wants will be. Once this happens, you will find that you are able to let go of all the "stuff" you used to want as part of the false image you created.

At one time I "wanted" all kinds of things: a fancy

car, a fancy house, beautiful clothes, the ability to stay at luxurious hotels and eat at expensive restaurants. I became attached to a lifestyle that seemed normal because of the environment in which I lived (the fast-paced life of a highly paid marketing executive in Silicon Valley). I bought into believing that I had to have all this stuff in my life so I could say that I was successful, that I had arrived. Through believing all this, I became a burned-out workaholic so that I could earn the money to have the stuff to convince myself I was living the good life.

At the time, it didn't seem out of whack at all. I had lots of money. I "wanted" for nothing. I had all these things, yet I had no time to enjoy them. I had no one with whom to share my "good life." I was empty and unhappy.

I did not dare think of leaving my job or taking a lower-paying one. I could not see that *this lifestyle owned me.* I built my jail cell, dug my burnout abyss filled with beautiful things that meant *absolutely nothing* to me.

There was no way I could see all this at the beginning of my breaking-through process. I could only sense that I had created a box and could not see my way out of it. As I began to take the steps you have just taken, I was gradually able to discern the full picture of just what I had done to myself.

As my needs were fully met, I no longer needed

"retail therapy" to make me feel better. I no longer needed to eat in fancy restaurants or stay at expensive hotels to prove I was successful, to myself or to anyone else. Instead I discovered that my greatest need was to have the *freedom to choose* what to do with my life. *Choice* was what I needed most.

For me, creating that choice meant getting my financial house in order. Beside paying bills on time, I began to save enough money so that I could live comfortably for six months without a job. I did that because I had no clue what I wanted to do next, but I did know that being forced every day to go to a job that I loathed was not it. In fairness to the company I worked for at the time, this was not about how they did or did not treat me. This was about creating a sense of financial security so that I could *choose* what I wanted.

The more financial security I had, the more choices I could see for myself. I could stay at that company and continue working (and it was amazing how much better I felt about my job because I no longer *had* to do it). I could take a different job in the same company. I could go to work for another company. I could start a new career and teach. I could go to school. I could become a consultant. The range and breadth of my choices became overwhelming. It seemed that opportunities appeared magically out of nowhere!

When you are burned out, it is tempting just to go

out and find another job because you are angry and frustrated with your work, your colleagues, etc., rather than stay and fix what's "broken." Your anger is magnified and blown out of proportion because you feel trapped in your job, but changing jobs just means changing jail cells. You haven't solved the problem.

You also allow your boundaries to be violated when you are feeling financially threatened (in danger of losing a job). As a result, you are probably not as much of a risk-taker in your work and in the decisions you make there. You don't want to lose your job because you are afraid to rock the boat, yet rocking the boat is sometimes exactly what the company needs! Instead, you wind up biting your tongue and then complaining to everyone else later.

Would you consider yourself to be in integrity in these circumstances: being in debt, living beyond your means, unable to do the right things because you might lose your job?

I want you to be able to see as many opportunities as possible and to have the freedom to choose what you want to do with your life.

> **REQUEST:** Put your financial house in order so you can have greater freedom and choice.

For one month, track how you spend your money. Yes, I know this is a pain in the neck, but the reality is that unless you do this you will kid yourself about how and on what you really spend your money. We're all good at conveniently forgetting little splurges such as that cup of designer coffee on the way to work.

I found that writing everything down served three purposes. One: I tracked all my expenses easily. Two: I could hand in my expense reports faster! Three: When I began working for myself, this behavior had become such a habit that it greatly simplified my taxes each year.

Pay yourself first. Yes, that's right. You worked hard for that money, and if you don't pay yourself, no one else will. Do this by contributing the maximum amount you can from every paycheck to your 401(K), IRA, or other investment vehicle. Have it taken right out of your salary and immediately deposited into your account so you are not even tempted to spend it. Also save 10% of your check each week or month so that within one year (or sooner) you will have at least six months of living expenses put away.

Pay yourself *before* you pay your bills. I know it sounds weird. I know it feels uncomfortable. Just do it! (It works!)

When I was working in the corporate world, I had always made the 401(K)/IRA contribution, but I had never before put away the extra 10% for living-expense savings. Once I did that and built up a financial reserve sufficient for six months of expenses, I was a completely different person. You can be too! Imagine what your life would be like with six months of expenses put away? How would you be different?

Locate a good financial advisor, and get rid of any credit card debt you have. Many of the consumer credit bureaus are very helpful in creating financial plans to help you eliminate your credit card debt. Some even offer additional financial services such as advising you about where to invest your savings. Here are some immediate actions to take:

- List every credit card you have, how much money you owe, the minimum payment, and the interest rate. Pay the minimum payment on all but the one with the highest interest rate. You must begin to pay more than the minimum payment on that one each month. Instead of buying that cup of designer coffee every day, add up how much you spend on frivolous expenditures every month, and add that extra amount to this high-interest credit card's monthly payment. Pay off that card, then add together the amount you were paying on it each month, plus the next card's minimum payment, and pay all of that to the next-highest-interest account on the list. Keep going until you have them all paid off.

• As you pay off each card, cut it up and toss it out. Do this until you have only the card with the lowest interest rate left. Put it in a drawer, and use it only for emergencies. Pay your bills and make in-store purchases only with cash or checks. For online and telephone purchases, use only e-checks or debit-type cards.

Reduce your living expenses to a level where you are comfortable and not suffering. Do you really need a cell phone? After all, what did you do before you had one...you did just fine, didn't you? Perhaps you feel you need one for emergencies. In that case, consider canceling your land-line phone and using only the cell.

Instead of eating out two or three times a week, why not initiate a rotating potluck dinner among friends. In addition, you can make cooking at home a family event. Dining at home with friends and family can be more relaxed and fun than eating out, and it's healthier for two reasons: eating fresh, healthful, home-cooked food and being with emotionally supportive loved ones. Both nourish you! Clip and use coupons for your groceries, and/or join a co-op.

What else can you do? **In your Travel Log, make a list of ten ways you will reduce your expenses, and do them immediately.** Create your budget, and stick with it.

Stop tempting yourself with retail therapy. Go shopping *only* if there's a specific item you *must* purchase. Decide how much you will spend before you go to the store, and stick within that limit. Leave as soon as you have made the purchase. Do not spend time with people who use retail therapy to soothe themselves. The last thing you need is encouragement to spend money on doodads that you rationalize into "needs."

Educate yourself about money. Pick up at least two books about managing money, and read them from cover to cover. (See the *Resources* section for suggestions of good money-books.) George Bernard Shaw once said "The *lack* of money is the root of all evil." How true!

None of us can live without money, and more money can mean greater freedom. The more you know about how to manage your money, how to take responsibility for your money, and what to do or not to do with it, the more choices and more freedom you will have in your life. The more educated you become about money, the more control and less fear you will have regarding earning it and managing it.

Most people do not need a lot of money to live comfortably. What you do need is to balance your income and expenses at a level that gives you the **freedom of choice.**

Be Inspired

> **Without the aid of the divine,**
> **man cannot walk even an inch.**
> —Chinese proverb

The dictionary defines *inspire* this way: *1. To breathe or blow into or upon; 2. to infuse (as life) by breathing, to inhale; 3. to exert an animating, enlivening or exalting influence on; 4. to draw forth or bring out; 5. to bring about.*

Wow! What would it be like if *you felt inspired all the time*? Who would you be? What could you accomplish?

Inspiration is one of the two healthiest, most easily renewable and effortless energy sources (love is the other). Being inspired means that you will find life joyful and meaningful. Being inspired means that you will never want for passion. Finding one or more sources of inspiration is your first step into the light.

I was finally able to get to this point in my own journey because I could fully *feel* again. I had allowed myself to be more vulnerable, more open. I could let my heart be touched and not be afraid. My heart felt new, raw, and exposed. I was able to let my heart speak for me and guide me. How incredibly wonderful it was to *feel* again, even if what I sometimes felt was sadness or pain.

After I was able to find and tap into my sources of inspiration, I knew I had recovered from burnout because my life became effortless and full of gratitude and satisfaction. I rediscovered my connection to the ocean and how deeply it fed my soul. (Whenever I stand on the shore to watch the waves roll and crash, I feel both insignificant and cherished at the same time.) I am also inspired by kindness, any kindness I observe, especially between strangers. I am inspired by the love I see between parent and child, husband and wife, siblings, friends, lovers. I am inspired whenever respect is shown by one for another. I am touched by planet Earth and marvel that this mere speck of dirt within such a vast universe can support such an amazing variety and quantity of life.

Most of all, *you* inspire me! Your dedication and willingness to care for yourself and love yourself so much that you have become healthier, stronger, and happier is an extraordinary gift to the universe.

From all this inspiration came the vision for my business and its mission, my passion for helping people to conquer burnout, my commitment to leading a life of integrity and serenity, my desire to give back to the universe what I have learned.

Now is the time for you to look around and discover what it is that inspires you, what you *value* deeply, so that you too can tap into that effortless, unbelievably powerful and healthy energy!

> **REQUEST:** Describe in your Travel Log moments you remember when you felt deeply touched or an event which occurred that caused you to change something about yourself in your life.

Maybe it was a speech you heard given by someone famous. ("I Have a Dream..." still gives me shivers.) Perhaps it was a scene in a movie or even the whole movie! ("Remember the Titans," "Gladiator," "Men of Honor," "Beaches," "Steel Magnolias," and "Ghandi" are some of my favorites.)

Did someone once say something to you that blew you away? (My niece told me to bring back "something from your heart" when asked what she wanted from Italy.) Did you visit a place that just took your breath away? (I believe that God lives in Yosemite National Park, if he resides anywhere specific.) Perhaps you saw a beautiful work of art? (Michelangelo does it for me every time.) Heard a brilliant piece of music? (Tchaikovsky's Piano Concerto #1 transports me to a very special place.)

Having trouble recognizing what truly inspires you? You will be able to tell when you feel inspired because you will feel a surge of energy from deep within you. You may feel excited, but the energy is more subtle than the type of excitement that's adrenaline-based. It isn't manic, always looking to *do* something. It has a joyous, glowing quality, and it allows you to spend time just *being*.

Ask others who know you well for their impressions of what they have noticed that inspires you. The best people to ask are those who have known you for a very long time. They can usually remember a wider variety of moments when they saw you fully engaged and inspired. Capture what they tell you in your Travel Log.

Review everything about who and what inspires you. What did your special moments have in common? What feelings did they evoke? What do those experiences represent for you? What themes or patterns appeared?

In any of those moments, were there people who deeply affected how you thought or felt, perhaps made you see things in a different light? What happened? What did they say or do? What was it that they touched in you? What did they inspire you to do? How are you different because of those experiences and people?

As you do this, to which sections or points do you find yourself most drawn?

List five things that inspire you in your Travel Log. Set aside time to experience those things on a regular basis, once a week at minimum. Do the things on your list so you can experience what inspires you or be with people who inspire you. For example, sit in an outdoor café and observe people, or play a musical instrument. Create opportunities, if necessary (plan dinner parties, take trips, purchase season tickets, etc.).

I listen to my favorite composers while I'm working in my office. I turn the volume down when I take phone calls, but music is constantly playing, so I am always inspired and soothed. I also go walking outdoors. Walking is a fabulous activity because it gives me the chance to be in nature and experience the trees, the flowers, the birds. It never ceases to amaze me how many shades of green there are. Green just may be God's favorite color!

I paint. Thanks to my husband's thoughtfulness in providing me with a portable easel and stool, I am able to go anywhere that strikes my fancy and immerse myself while I attempt to recreate the beauty I experience.

Inspiration can move mountains.
Inspiration can change the world.
Inspiration can transform you.

Be inspired, and you can achieve anything!

Life After Burnout

Stressed souls need the reassuring
rhythm of self-nurturing rituals.
—Sarah Ban Breathnach

How excited you must be to reach this page! Today is the first day of your life After Burnout (A. B.)!

You have emerged from your self-created jail cell or dungeon. Today you step fully into the light to embrace your new life. Today is the day when you declare, "My life is *mine*! I will treat it with respect, I will honor it, I will treasure it, and I will *never* again give it away!"

CONGRATULATIONS!

What an amazing journey you have made! You have gone from being a half-crazed, unhappy, frustrated, angry, exhausted person to becoming an incredibly strong, resilient, self-assured, relaxed, attractive one!

YOU DID IT!

You are not a caterpillar anymore. You are a butterfly!

Today is the perfect day for you to celebrate your freedom, to celebrate your new life. Today is also the day to begin putting into place some rituals and practices to maintain your freedom.

> **REQUEST:** Decide the perfect way to celebrate this magnificent accomplishment! Decide with whom you want to share this day and whom you wish to acknowledge your accomplishment.

Create a ceremony to communicate how important this achievement is to you. Remember the theme of your journey and the signs you hung up? What would best express that theme now: a poem, a song, a piece of literature, an excerpt from your Travel Log, a painting, a photograph, a sculpture, an everyday object in your home or workplace?

Would you like to read something suitable out loud? Create a document, burn it, and scatter the ashes? Write new lyrics to a tune you like? Go skydiving with friends, and carry a banner? Make it perfect *for you!*

The day I reached the light, when I could see that I was clear of this burnout thing and rejoiced in my hard-won and newly found freedom, I wanted to do a combination of things for myself. That day

I meditated, walked on the beach (of course!), played my favorite music on my piano, and then called each member of my support team and invited them out to their favorite restaurant. I also took my husband to our favorite getaway to thank him especially for all his love and support.

I've known other people who celebrated by doing something they had never done before— hiking in a forest, staying at a B&B with a significant loved-one, taking their first flying lesson, visiting a foreign country.

Do something that is meaningful to you so you can reward yourself for all your hard work and remember what an incredible achievement this is!

Pick a day and a time each month (mine is Saturday morning between eight and ten), when you check in with yourself to see how things are going. A monthly reflection will keep you aware and present so that you can more easily identify whether you may be falling back into the burnout cycle and take immediate action to stop it. To help you not to slip back into your old habits, this regular check-in time allows you to regroup and collect your thoughts. You can use this time to forgive yourself if you occasionally slip up (which you likely will from time to time) and also to guide yourself back on track.

I start my check-in by finding in a comfortable

spot. I try to sit in a place from which I can see something beautiful wherever I look. I make sure I am not too warm or too cold. I often play "Spectrum Suite" by Steven Halpern on my stereo in the background. I do deep-breathing exercises and gentle yoga stretches to relax my body. I send out a simple request to the Divine: "This is my time; this is my space. Allow me to receive what I need; allow me to give what I have to share." This lets me clear my mind and my body so I can feel what is there. I then use this checklist, which you are welcome to adapt for your own use:

- I review my physical health. How does my body feel? Is there any tension or discomfort? If my tummy is in knots, I'm worrying about something. I take the time to relax my tummy, figure out what is bothering me, and decide how I will take care of it.

- I clear myself of any lingering emotions I may have bottled up for the past month. I let myself feel each one—whether it's anger, guilt, sadness, joy, confusion…. I don't judge them (this is a good time to be wary of Wanda and make sure not to engage with her). I feel them fully, acknowledge them, and then let them go. The more often I do this, the better I become at just feeling without judgment, and the clearer I am able to think as a result.

- I review my Travel Log and remember what I am

grateful for—all the things, both "good" and "bad," that have happened in the past month to make me feel alive and grateful for my life.

- I check to see how I am spending my time and if that feels right to me. I note what level of attention I am giving to each facet of my life and make whatever adjustments I need so I am feeling more in tune. Some weeks I want more writing time; in others I want more house-care time; in still others I want more time with friends. I am constantly adjusting so that I'm flowing with my life instead of fighting it.

- I take a look at my integrity to see where I am okay and where I am not. Wherever I am not, I immediately resolve it.

- I reflect on how firm my boundaries and standards are. Have they been tested lately? (Somebody's always doing that!) Did they get stronger or weaker? If they're weaker, I seek out the root cause (this occasionally requires my coach to shine a big spotlight so I can see it), and I deal with it.

- I take some time to review my successes in the past month and celebrate them by writing them down in my Travel Log and then sharing them with the various people in my life who can appreciate them. I share my business successes with my husband, Allan, and with my dad; I share my creative successes with Allan, my dad, and my creative support team. I share my emotional successes with my coach (well, actually, she gets to hear about *all* of them), especially regarding standards and boundaries!

- I end by again calling upon the Divine: "Allow me to hear what I need to hear, to see what I need to see, to speak kindly and do kind things." Then I make one specific request that is particularly important to me at that moment.

Structure your reflection time and process in whatever ways work best for you. Use some of the time to reflect on the areas that were the most challenging for you during your burnout journey and, if you are comfortable with it, ask the Divine (or God, or whichever name you prefer to use) for guidance in solving this dilemma. Give yourself permission to adjust the structure until you find one that works easily. Not everyone wants to or needs to call on the Divine. I add this because without it my process would feel incomplete.

It can be relatively easy to fall back into the burnout cycle without being aware of it. After all, it took you a long time to become burned out and to get really good at it! It will take some time to develop a full set of necessary skills so you are even better at avoiding burning out again. From time to time you may feel you need some extra help. Should you want additional support to help you maintain your new-found freedom, you are welcome to join a *Break Free from Burnout* team. More information is available at the back of this book.

Welcome to your beautiful new life A. B.!

May your day be filled with blessings
Like the sun that lights the sky
And may you always have the courage
To spread your wings and fly!
—Irish Blessing

Tell Me Your Story

I want to hear about your successes, your challenges, and the insights you have discovered as a result of using the program in this book. I want to hear what you liked and what you did not like; what worked for you and what did not work for you; how you experimented and made something work for you; how you helped someone else, and how that helped you.

Be Featured on My Web Site

Over and over again, people tell me that what makes the biggest difference in how quickly they break free from burnout is hearing about other people's struggles and knowing that they are not alone out there. Your story can serve to inspire other individuals who are struggling with their own journey through burnout.

I would be honored to publish your story online. On my web site, I feature stories that rotate periodically—the experiences of my clients and of others who have read this book, taken the e-course, or attended one of my teleclasses, workshops, or retreats.

Shine a light on your achievement by telling us

what you have accomplished and how! Simply go to this web address, and fill out the form you find there:

http://www.maryplewis.com/btb/story.html

Don't forget to send me your picture, as well—the form will give you all the necessary instructions.

Resources

Here is a list of books, articles, and web sites that I have found useful over the years in my own and my clients' struggles with burnout. Many of these come from my clients' suggestions and explorations. I've included opinions where I have strong ones. All these books are available through Amazon.com or BarnesandNoble.com.

Adrenaline
Various articles and information on the web dealing with the various conditions than can come about as a result of adrenaline depletion. Some include baseline information about the adrenal glands.

- http://www.medhelp.org/nadf/frameset.html
- http://www.merck.com/pubs/mmanual_home/sec13/146.htm
- http://www.cc.nih.gov/ccc/patient_education/pepubs/mgnadrins.pdf
- http://www.cc.nigh.gov/medlineplus/adrenalgland disorders.html
- http://www.niddk.nih.gov/health/endo/pubs/addison/addison.htm

Attitude Adjustments
- *Attitude is Everything: 10 Life-Changing Steps to Turning Attitude into Action* by Keith Harrell

Boundaries / Standards / Integrity
- *Asserting Yourself* by Sharon Anthony Bower, Gordon H. Bower
- *Your Perfect Right: Assertiveness and Equality in Your Life and Relationships* (8th Edition) by Robert E. Alberti, Michael L. Emmons
- *Ethics for the New Millennium*, by His Holiness, the Dalai Lama. It doesn't matter what His Holiness writes, it's all incredible. You'll see more of his books listed elsewhere in the list. Each is a unique, life-altering experience. What an awe-inspiring human being he is!

Burnout
Various articles on the web that discuss burnout and offer other resources:
- http://www.aafp.org/fpm/970400fm/lead.html
- http://www.aafp.org/fpm/970300fm/balance.html
- http://www.coolware.com/health/medical_reporter/burnout.html

Burnout Coaching Teams
- If you would like to join a mutually supportive coaching team that includes others struggling with burnout, and also receive a monthly private coaching session, see: http://www.maryplewis.com/services.html

Career
- http://www.wetfeet.com offers information on various public companies, as well as career information and advice.
- http://www.highlandsprogram.com offers one of the better career assessments I've seen on the market. It provides a truly accurate assessment based on your natural talents and abilities, since it actually tests for them instead of relying on your opinion or others'. If you lack the vocabulary to describe what you do well; if you do not truly know what you do well; if you have little understanding of what work environment would make you blossom, this assessment is well worth the investment.
- http://www.keirsey.com, and http://www.advisorteam.com/user/ktsintro1.asp offer a personality assessment based on the Meyers-Briggs Personality Temperament Indicator. This test provides an excellent start to understanding your personality. Their free assessment is a good base. The $19.95 they charge for the full career-profile report is a good value.

Internet job boards for placing your resume, getting career information and advice:
- http://www.hotjobs.com
- http://www.monsterboard.com is the "big daddy" of them all. Which means you have to work consistently to keep your resume current and on top of the lists.
- http://www.6figures.com focuses on jobs with a

minimum annual salary of $100,000.
- http://www.headhunter.net targets recruiters who are looking for candidates for their clients' job openings.
- http://www.guru.com for consultants/contractors.
- http://www.sologig.com for consultants/contractors.
- *Pathfinder* by Nicholas Lore
- *Please Understand Me II* by David Keirsey. The foundation for the Keirsey temperament sorter. Excellent material to keep on hand.
- *Making A Life, Making A Living* by Mark Albion. "Dr. Mark," as he is fondly called by many, provides a wonderful perspective on how to maintain your values and your integrity while finding the right way for you to make a living.
- *First, Break All the Rules* by Marcus Buckingham and Curt Coffman

Community
- *Friendshifts : The Power of Friendship and How It Shapes Our Lives* by Jan Yager
- *Friendship Factor: How to Get Closer to the People You Care For* by Alan Loy McGinnis
- *Relationships: What It Takes to Be a Friend* by Pamela Reeve
- *How to Start a Conversation and Make Friends* by Don Gabor,
- *How to Be a People Magnet* by Leil Lowndes

Delegating
- *Delegating for Results* by Robert B. Maddux
- *Effective Delegation* by Chris Roebuck

Effective Meetings
- *First Aid for Meetings: Quick Fixes and Major Repairs for Running Effective Meetings* by Charlie Hawkins
- *How to Make Meetings Work* by Michael Doyle, David Straus

Energy Vampires
- *Toxic People: 10 Ways of Dealing With People Who Make Your Life Miserable* by Lillian Glass
- *Emotional Blackmail: When the People in Your Life Use Fear, Obligation and Guilt to Manipulate You* by Susan Forward, Donna Frazier

Fear
- *Feel the Fear and Do It Anyway* by Susan Jeffers
- *Inner Talk for Peace of Mind* by Susan Jeffers
- *Living Courageously in a Changing World: 101 Tips for Authentic Success* by Judy Irving. This is the only title not available through standard distribution channels. You can order it from Judy directly at: http://www.movingon.net. It is a delightful book filled with all kinds of good tips and ways to build up your courage muscle.
- *What to Say When You Talk to Yourself* by Shad Helmstetter
- *Self Talk: Key to Personal Growth* by David A. Stoop

- *The Dark Side of the Light Chasers* by Debbie Ford

Fear of Being in Deep Water

- The Transpersonal Swimming Institute: http://www.conquerfear.com I cannot recommend this group highly enough. Founder and CEO Melon Dash has developed a groundbreaking technique that is fabulously effective to help adults overcome their fear of deep water. I feel as though I am a poster child for them! After more than forty years of being terrified even to get my face wet in the shower, I was floating comfortably on my back in one night, and within six months I became a certified open-water scuba diver. It is truly miraculous! Don't let yourself, or someone you love, miss out on the joy of playing freely and confidently in the water. TSI has a video you can buy to see what it's all about and offers classes all across the U.S. Melon asked the Gallup polling organization to conduct a survey of U.S. adults, resulting in the astounding finding that almost 60% of Americans experience some level of anxiety while in deep water. You likely know at least one person who is afraid of being in the water. Do a good deed and pass this information along to them!

Finances/Money

- *Rich Dad, Poor Dad* by Robert Kiyosaki
- *Cashflow Quadrant: Rich Dad's Guide to Financial Freedom* by Robert Kiyosaki. This book literally changed my entire perspective on making money!

All of a sudden, the light bulbs went on and stayed on! If financial independence is at all appealing to you, I strongly recommend that you buy this one...and lots of highlighters.

- *Retire Young, Retire Rich* by Robert Kiyosaki
- *9 Steps to Financial Freedom* by Suze Orman
- *The Courage to Be Rich* by Suze Orman
- *Multiple Streams of Income* by Robert G. Allen
- *The Millionaire Next Door* by Thomas J. Stanley
- http://www.richdad.com Robert Kiyosaki's web site that is full of great information including products not available anywhere else such as his Cashflow 101 game. If you want to rewire your head for financial independence, the game is worth the price tag.
- http://www.leapsystems.com is a performance-based financial planning service recommended by Robert Kiyosaki.
- http://www.fpanet.org is another financial planners association.
- http://www.napfa.org is a fee-only financial advisers association.
- http://www.motleyfool.com is an excellent Web site for learning about the world of investing and finance.
- http://www.fidelity.com is the site for one of the world's largest mutual fund / investment firms, with tons of information about investing.
- http://www.cfp-board.org is the Certified Financial Planner's association site, where you can learn about what they do and how to find a CFP near you.
- http://www.multiplestreamsofincome.com is

Robert G. Allen's web site, where he offers lots of
information and free seminars. Beware: Once you
sign up for his free newsletters or seminars, you will
be deluged with junk mail from other organizations
to whom he sells his mailing list. If you
subscribe/register to anything, do it with an e-mail
address you don't use often, such as a hotmail.com
or yahoo.com email account.

Find a Coach
**Any of these free coach referral services can
help you locate the right coach for you.**
- http://www.coachvillereferral.com is a free coach-
  referral service from Coachville, a professional
  association / training organization for coaches. Many
  coaches' listings also include sound-bytes so you can
  hear what the coaches sound like! This is a very nice
  way to get to know someone before you call.
- http://www.coachreferral.com is a free coach-referral
  service from Coach University, the largest accredited
  coach training organization.
- http://www.coachfederation.org/aboutcoaching/find-
  acoach.htm is a free coach-referral service from
  another professional coach association, the ICF
  (International Coach Federation).

Inspiration / Spirituality
- *Sacred Contracts* by Carolyn Myss. This is a superb
  book to help you figure out what your purpose is on
  the Earth in this lifetime. It's not an easy book to

read, but well worth going through the process if this is something that you wonder about or that has eluded you.

- *Why People Don't Heal and How They Can* by Carolyn Myss. One of my most favorite books that gets right to the heart of what Carolyn terms "woundology", a tacitly condoned behavior of hanging on to wounds. Well worth the read. She's also an incredibly talented speaker and workshop leader. If you ever have the inclination and the opportunity to attend a talk or go to her workshop—do it!
- *The Four Agreements: A Practical Guide to Personal Freedom* by Don Miguel Ruiz. An excellent book that is a quick, pleasurable read, this is one that you will read again and again.
- *Authentic Power: Aligning Personality with Soul* by Gary Zukav
- *The Heart of the Soul: Emotional Awareness* by Gary Zukav, Linda Francis
- *The Heart Aroused* by David Whyte. This is a must-read if you work in any type of organization. Get the book AND spring for the audiotapes or CD. David Whyte is a bard in the true bardic tradition. He uses his voice and poetry to uncover so much of what we hide deep within ourselves. You will have no defense against this great bard and poet. His mission of bringing the heart and soul back into organizations is best experienced by listening to him. If you ever have the opportunity to hear him speak live, do so!

- *The Seat of the Soul* by Gary Zukav
- *Igniting Your Soul Life* by Gary Zukav, Michael Toms (Contributor), Jill Kramer
- *How to Practice: The Way to a Meaningful Life* by His Holiness, the Dalai Lama, Jeffrey Hopkins (Translator)
- *An Open Heart: Practicing Compassion in Everyday Life* by the Dalai Lama, Nicholas Vreeland (Editor)

Management / Leadership

- *Results-Based Leadership* by David Ullrich, Jack Zenger, and Norm Smallwood. This is an incredibly advanced, definitive, and wonderful book on what I have personally found to be the most insightful work on leadership in the last 20 years. A must-read for anyone aspiring to true leadership.
- *The One Minute Manager* by Ken Blanchard. This classic book is an excellent primer for beginning managers.
- *The One Minute Manager Meets the Monkey* by William Oncken Jr. and Ken Blanchard. This book is a good primer to help beginning managers get past some of the challenges of managing themselves and their workloads.
- *Leadership and the One Minute Manager: Increasing Effectiveness Through Situational Leadership* by Patricia Zigarmi, et al. A further extension of the original One Minute Manager, applying rudimentary principles of leadership.
- *The One Minute Manager Builds High Performing Teams* by Ken Blanchard, et al

Perfection / Perfectionism
- *The Care and Feeding of Perfectionists* by Cynthia Curnan
- *When Perfect Isn't Good Enough: Strategies for Coping with Perfectionism* by Martin M. Antony, Richard P. Swinson

Saying No
- *201 Ways to Say No Effectively and Gracefully* by Alan Axelrod, Jim Holtje, James Holtje. This is a handy guide for those times when you are struggling for the right words to say in a pinch.
- *Difficult Conversations: How to Discuss What Matters Most* by Douglas Stone, Bruce Patton, Sheila Heen, Roger Fisher
- *Don't Say Yes When You Want to Say No* by Herbert Fensterheim
- *When I Say No, I Feel Guilty* by Manuel J. Smith
- *When I Say No I Feel Guilty, Vol. II, for Managers and Executives* by Manuel J. Smith

Sleep
- *The Promise of Sleep: A Pioneer in Sleep Medicine Explores the Vital Connection Between Health, Happiness, and a Good Night's Sleep* by William C. Dement, Christopher Vaughan. Check this out of the library; don't buy it unless you really intend to become a sleep disorder expert. It's a fantastic introduction to the topic and will give you sufficient information to guide you in the questions to ask

your immediate health care provider and the sleep disorder specialist you may choose to consult.

- http://www.sleepdisorders.com is an excellent web site to help you learn about the various types of sleep disorders, with links to excellent resources.
- http://www.sleepnet.com/ is another really good resource for learning about sleep disorders, with various chat forums.
- http://www.whatsthebest-mattress.com/ is a great resource to help you determine what kind of mattress is best for you.
- http://www.selectcomfort.com/ This bed manufacturer produces air mattresses that can be customized on each side at any given moment, so couples can have separate firmness settings.
- http://www.flou.qc.ca/where.html This is another bed manufacturer that offers a different concept with integrated linens, mattresses, bases, and headboards.
- http://www.cuddledown.com A wonderful purveyor of bed linens, dust-mite proof mattress, pillow case and duvet covers. They custom design and make sheets, pillows and other linens for you. Nice people and excellent customer service.

Time Management / Organizing Yourself
- *Time Management from the Inside Out* by Julia Morgenstern
- *Organizing from the Inside Out* by Julia Morgenstern
- *Checklists for Life : 104 Lists to Help You Get*

Organized, Save Time, and Unclutter Your Life by
Kirsten M. Lagatree
- *The Procrastinator's Handbook: Mastering the Art of Doing It Now* by Rita Emmett
- http://www.assistu.com is an excellent place to find a virtual assistant. Virtual assistants provide many standard administrative services such as scheduling appointments. handling your books and correspondence as well as more technical or sophisticated activities such as designing and maintaining web sites.
- http://www.napo.net is the National Association of Professional Organizers' web site where you can find an organizer near you to help clean out those closets, organize your desk, etc., etc.

Index

About the Author

Mary Planding Lewis enjoys coaching executives, business owners, managers, entrepreneurs, and creative geniuses to help them improve their personal and professional lives dramatically and profoundly. Her direct, playful, and challenging coaching style provides the clarity, structure, and support her clients demand and utilize to reach heights they never before imagined.

A graduate of Coach University and former Chair of the International Coach Federation's (ICF) Technology Standards and Practices Committee, Mary was the first publisher of the ICF *Organizational Coach eJournal*. She has been coaching since the late nineties. She conducts retreats and workshops on how to beat burnout, and her *"Creating and Living Your Perfect Life"* retreats are held at spas and health resorts internationally.

A twenty-year marketing veteran of the high-tech and Internet industries, Mary has worked at Fortune-500 firms and startups on both coasts of the U.S. A native New Yorker, she came to Silicon Valley in the early eighties and now resides on the central coast of California (when she and her husband aren't traveling in their RV). She holds an

MBA from San Jose State University and a BA in French and German from the State University of New York at Binghamton.

Mary provides individual and group coaching and regularly leads workshops and retreats. For more information on services she provides, view her web site at **http://www.maryplewis.com** where you may also subscribe to her free newsletter.

Share *Break Free from Burnout* with Others

To order copies of this book, go to:
http://www.maryplewis.com or call 1-866-MARY-LEWIS

Special discounts are also available on bulk purchases for sales promotions, premiums, fundraising, or education use.

Order Form for individual customers only (1-25 copies)

Payable in US funds only. Book price: $14.95 each copy.
Postage and handling are extra. CA residents will pay sales tax.
We accept *VISA and MasterCard* only. No cash/COD or checks.
Call 1-866-MARY-LEWIS, or fax your order to 1-831-438-3361,
or mail it to: The Marketing Clinic,
245M Mt. Hermon Rd., #209, Scotts Valley, CA 95066

Bill My Credit Card # _____ **Exp. Date:** _____

Cardholder Signature: _____

Bill to: _____

Address: _____

City: _____

State/Prov.: _____ Zip/Postal Code: _____

Country: _____ Daytime Phone #: _____

E-mail address: _____

Quantity (1-25 books): _____ Book Total (_____ x $14.95) _____

(CA residents only) Add Applicable Sales Tax _____

Postage and Handling _____

(US/Can. $3.50 for one book, $1.00 for each additional)

TOTAL Amount Due US $ _____

Ship to: _____

Address: _____

City: _____

State/Prov.: _____ Zip/Postal Code: _____

Country: _____ Daytime Phone #: _____

Please allow 4-6 weeks for US delivery. Canada/International orders,
please allow 8-10 weeks. Price and offer are subject to change without notice.

You Don't Have to Go It Alone!

Join a "Break Free" Team, and Get a Free Monthly 30-minute Private Coaching Session with Mary Lewis*

Let's face it: Some of us simply lack the steadfastness to complete certain tasks on our own; we're just not wired that way. Many of us enjoy sharing activities with others because we get more done. Some may also lack a solid, reliable, personal support system to help get them through.

If any of these descriptions fits you, a *Break Free* team may be the answer. Team members provide each other with information and support as we break free from our burnout cycles AND as we move forward into creating more meaningful and fulfilling lives.

How does it work? Team members are asked to make a three-month commitment so that mutual trust and intimacy can develop. We meet twice a month on the phone by calling in to a special telephone number. Mary Lewis, coach and burnout survivor, leads our group discussion and is there to guide us when we need or request it. To allow for sufficient individual attention, teams include a maximum of 24 members. Mary also provides unlimited e-mail support to the team. A minimum of four members may create a team, and new teams are forming continually. There's certain to be a team whose meeting day and time fits into your calendar!

*As part of your membership, Mary will include a free

monthly 30-minute private coaching session for as long as you are a member of a *Break Free* team.

Cost is US $150 per month.

Mary offers a 100% Satisfaction Guarantee:

"If you decide that your *Break Free* team membership is not effective for you, whether because the team format isn't working for you or because you feel that the team environment isn't delivering what you need, you may resign at any time, and I will refund 100% of the current month's membership fees. All I ask is that you send me an e-mail outlining one thing that I should/could have done differently to have been of greater assistance. Upon request, I will also be happy to provide you with the names of other coaches to contact if you would like to continue the coaching process with someone else."

You've got nothing to lose!

Call 1-866-MARY-LEWIS,
email: info@maryplewis.com, or visit
http://www.maryplewis.com/services.html
to sign up.

Price and offer are subject to change without notice.